The Revels Plays
COMPANION LIBRARY

SUSAN BROCK, SUSAN CERASANO, PETER CORBIN, E. A. J. HONIGMANN,
GRACE IOPPOLO, J. R. MULRYNE and ROBERT SMALLWOOD
former editors

For more than half a century *The Revels Plays* have offered the most authoritative editions of Elizabethan and Jacobean plays by authors other than Shakespeare. The *Companion Library* provides a fuller background to the main series by publishing important dramatic and non-dramatic material that will be essential for the serious student of the period.

Three seventeenth-century plays on women and performance
eds CHALMERS, SANDERS & TOMLINSON
Doing Kyd: A collection of essays on The Spanish Tragedy ed. CINPOEŞ
'Art made tongue-tied by authority' CLARE
Drama of the English Republic, 1649–60 CLARE
Three Jacobean witchcraft plays eds CORBIN, SEDGE
The Stukeley Plays ed. EDELMAN
Three Renaissance usury plays ed. KERMODE
Beyond The Spanish Tragedy: *A study of the works of Thomas Kyd* ERNE
Three sixteenth-century dietaries ed. FITZPATRICK
John Ford's political theatre HOPKINS
The works of Richard Edwards KING
Marlowe and the popular tradition: Innovation in the English drama before 1595 LUNNEY
Banquets set forth: Banqueting in English Renaissance drama MEADS
Thomas Heywood: Three marriage plays ed. MERCHANT
Three romances of Eastern conquest ed. NIAYESH
Three Renaissance travel plays ed. PARR
John Lyly PINCOMBE
A textual companion to Doctor Faustus RASMUSSEN
Documents of the Rose Playhouse RUTTER
John Lyly: Euphues: The Anatomy of Wit *and* Euphues and His England
ed. SCRAGG
John Lyly: Pap with an Hatchet, *An annotated, modern-spelling edition* SCRAGG
Richard Brome: Place and politics on the Caroline stage STEGGLE

Five Elizabethan progress entertainments

Manchester University Press

THE REVELS PLAYS COMPANION LIBRARY

Five Elizabethan progress entertainments

AN ANNOTATED
MODERN-SPELLING EDITION

Leah Scragg

Manchester University Press

Copyright © Leah Scragg 2019

The right of Leah Scragg to be identified as the author of this work has been asserted by her in accordance with the Copyright, Designs and Patents Act 1988.

Published by Manchester University Press
Altrincham Street, Manchester M1 7JA, UK
www.manchesteruniversitypress.co.uk

British Library Cataloguing-in-Publication Data is available

ISBN 978 1 5261 0947 7 hardback
ISBN 978 1 5261 0948 4 paperback

First published by Manchester University Press in hardback 2019

This edition published 2021

The publisher has no responsibility for the persistence or accuracy of URLs for any external or third-party internet websites referred to in this book, and does not guarantee that any content on such websites is, or will remain, accurate or appropriate.

Typeset by Toppan Best-set Premedia Limited

CONTENTS

GENERAL EDITORS' PREFACE	*page* vi
ACKNOWLEDGEMENTS	vii
ABBREVIATIONS	ix
INTRODUCTION: THE ROYAL PROGRESS	1
THE ENTERTAINMENT AT COWDRAY	17
Introduction	18
Text	29
THE ENTERTAINMENT AT ELVETHAM	45
Introduction	47
Text	58
THE ENTERTAINMENT AT BISHAM	91
Introduction	92
Text	101
THE ENTERTAINMENT AT MITCHAM	109
Introduction	110
Text	117
Appendix	128
THE ENTERTAINMENT AT CHISWICK	131
Introduction	132
Text	136
INDEX	139

GENERAL EDITORS' PREFACE

Since the late 1950s the series known as The Revels Plays has provided for students of the English Renaissance drama carefully edited texts of the major Elizabethan and Jacobean plays. The series includes some of the best-known drama of the period and has continued to expand, both within its original field and, to a lesser extent, beyond it, to include some important plays from the earlier Tudor and from the Restoration periods. The Revels Plays Companion Library is intended to further this expansion and to allow for new developments.

The aim of the Companion Library is to provide students of the Elizabethan and Jacobean drama with a fuller sense of its background and context. The series includes volumes of a variety of kinds. Small collections of plays, by a single author or concerned with a single theme and edited in accordance with the principles of textual modernisation of The Revels Plays, offer a wider range of drama than the main series can include. Together with editions of masques, pageants and the non-dramatic work of Elizabethan and Jacobean playwrights, these volumes make it possible, within the overall Revels enterprise, to examine the achievements of the major dramatists from a broader perspective. Other volumes provide a fuller context for the plays of the period by offering new collections of documentary evidence on Elizabethan theatrical conditions and on the performance of plays during that period and later. A third aim of the series is to offer modern critical interpretation, in the form of collections of essays or of monographs, of the dramatic achievement of the English Renaissance.

So wide a range of material necessarily precludes the standard format and uniform general editorial control which is possible in the original series of Revels Plays. To a considerable extent, therefore, treatment and approach are determined by the needs and intentions of individual volume editors. Within this rather ampler area, however, we hope that the Companion Library maintains the standards of scholarship that have for so long characterised The Revels Plays, and that it offers a useful enlargement of the work of the series in preserving, illuminating and celebrating the drama of Elizabethan and Jacobean England.

ACKNOWLEDGEMENTS

This modern-spelling collection of Elizabethan progress entertainments is heavily dependent on two previous old-spelling editions markedly different from one another in scope. The revision of John Nichols's *The Progresses and Public Processions of Queen Elizabeth I* (1823), published under the general editorship of Elizabeth Goldring, Faith Eales, Elizabeth Clarke, and Jayne Elisabeth Archer in five volumes by Oxford University Press in 2014, has made the wealth of information assembled by Nichols available to scholars in readily researchable form, enabling access to a vast number of freshly edited texts and up-to-date information. By contrast, Leslie Hotson's *Queen Elizabeth's Entertainment at Mitcham* (Yale Elizabethan Club, New Haven and London, 1953), a much more modest edition of only 57 pages and a print-run of 500 copies, contains only two short pieces, but it has nevertheless proved invaluable for the present project, in that neither item has been published elsewhere. I am indebted to the former at numerous points throughout this edition, and to the latter for a reliable transcription of the last two items included here.

I also owe a considerable debt of gratitude to three, in particular, of the many friends and colleagues who have come to my assistance in the course of this work. From the outset of my engagement with the *Entertainment at Elvetham* I have benefited from the advice and support of H. Neville Davies, whose investigations led to the discovery of a copy of the supposedly lost second quarto in the Royal Library at Windsor, and thence to the publication, in the revised Nichols, of the only authoritative edition of the work. Though primary materials and other editions were consulted, the text of *Elvetham* presented here is chiefly dependent on his work, and its greater reliability in comparison with other modern-spelling editions is largely attributable to him. Any errors, however, are entirely my own.

Throughout the history of my engagement with the editing of early modern texts I have relied upon the classical learning of Robin Griffin to supplement my little Latin and less Greek. As always, he brought his unflagging enthusiasm and commitment to the present project, and I am conscious that my annotation of a number of passages (in *Elvetham*, in particular) would have been considerably less informative but for his help. It is a great pleasure to have this opportunity to thank him for all his researches on my behalf over a considerable number of years, and to record my gratitude for his patience in responding to the most trivial of enquiries.

To Martin Wiggins, as on many previous occasions, I am indebted for his promptness in responding to a host of requests, from appeals for information to supplying reproductions of early modern texts. It is the busiest people, in my experience, who are often the most generous with their time.

My interest in progress entertainments was initially stirred by the extraordinary events staged on and around the artificial lake constructed at Elvetham for the Queen's visit in 1591. I would like to record my gratitude to the staff at the Royal Library at Windsor, who assisted me in securing permission to reproduce the celebrated site map of the event, published as a fold-out leaf in the second quarto in 1591 (Royal Collection Trust / copyright Her Majesty Queen Elizabeth II, 2017, RCIN 1024755).

My thanks are also due to the staff of the Northamptonshire Record Office and the British Library who enabled me to access materials pertaining to the entertainments at Chiswick and Mitcham.

ABBREVIATIONS

ABBREVIATIONS USED IN THE NOTES

ed.	edition /editor
HT	head-title
MS	manuscript
OED	*Oxford English Dictionary*
pub.	publisher
Q1	first quarto
Q2	second quarto
Qq	quartos
rev.	revised
SD	stage direction
SN	side-note
SP	speech prefix
subst.	substantively
vol.	volume

EDITIONS AND CRITICAL WORKS

The place of publication is London unless otherwise indicated. All references to the works of Shakespeare are to *The Arden Shakespeare Complete Works*, general eds Richard Proudfoot, Ann Thompson, and David Scott Kastan (1998, rev. 2001). Abbreviations of the titles of Shakespeare's plays are those adopted by The Revels Plays. References to other early modern plays are to the Revels editions, unless otherwise stated. Citations of classical works are to the most recent volumes in the Loeb Classical Library series. All references to the Bible are to the Authorized Version (1611).

Anatomy of Wit   *Euphues: The Anatomy of Wit*. See Lyly.
Barnes   Joseph Barnes, *Speeches deliuered to Her Maiestie this last Progresse, at the Right Honorable the Lady Russels, at Bissam, the Right Honorable the Lorde Chandos at Sudley, at the Right Honorable the Lord Norris, at Ricorte* (1592).
Bisham   *The Entertainment at Bisham*.
Bond   R. Warwick Bond, ed., *The Complete Works of John Lyly*, 3 vols (Oxford, 1902, reprinted 1967, 1973).
Butler   Katherine Butler, *Music in Elizabethan Court Politics* (Woodbrige, 2015).
Campaspe   See Lyly.
Chambers   E.K. Chambers, *The Elizabethan Stage*, 4 vols (Oxford, 1923, reprinted 1965).
Chiswick   *The Entertainment at Chiswick*.
Cowdray   *The Entertainment at Cowdray*.
Davies   H. Neville Davies, 'Looking Again at Elvetham: An Elizabethan Entertainment Revisited', in Margaret Shewring and Linda Briggs,

	eds, *Waterborne Pageants and Festivities in the Renaissance: Essays in Honour of J.R. Mulryne* (Farnham, 2013), pp. 211–42.
Elvetham	*The Entertainment at Elvetham.*
England	*Euphues and His England.* See Lyly.
Galatea	See Lyly.
Hent	William Wright (pub.), *The Honorable Entertainment Giuen to the Queenes Maiestie in Progresse, at Cowdrey in Sussex* (1591).
Hotson	Leslie Hotson, ed., *Queen Elizabeth's Entertainment at Mitcham*, Yale Elizabethan Club (New Haven and London, 1953).
Kinney	Arthur F. Kinney, ed., *Rennaissance Drama; An Anthology of Plays and Entertainments* (Malden, MA, and Oxford, 1999).
Lyly	All references to the work of John Lyly are to The Revels Plays, Revels Student editions, and Revels Plays Companion Library series (Manchester): *Euphues: The Anatomy of Wit* and *Euphues and His England* in Leah Scragg, ed., *Euphues: The Anatomy of Wit* and *Euphues and His England* (2003); *Campaspe* and *Sappho and Phao* in George K. Hunter and David Bevington, eds, *Campaspe* and *Sappho and Phao* (1991); *Galatea*, ed. Leah Scragg (2012); *Midas* in George. K. Hunter and David Bevington, eds, *Galatea* and *Midas* (2000); *Mother Bombie*, ed., Leah Scragg (2010); *The Woman in the Moon*, ed., Leah Scragg (2006); *Pap with an Hatchet*, ed. Leah Scragg (2015).
Midas	See Lyly.
Mitcham	*The Entertainment at Mitcham.*
Mother Bombie	See Lyly.
Nichols	John Nichols, *The Progresses and Public Processions of Queen Elizabeth I* (1788–1823), rev. Elizabeth Goldring, Faith Eales, Elizabeth Clarke, Jayne Elisabeth Archer (general eds), 5 vols (Oxford, 2014).
Progresses	Jayne Elisabeth Archer, Elizabeth Goldring, and Sarah Knight, eds, *The Progresses, Pageants, and Entertainments of Queen Elizabeth I* (Oxford, 2007, reprinted 2010).
Shent	William Wright (pub.), *The Speeches and Honorable Entertainment Giuen to the Queenes Maiestie in Progresse, at Cowdrey in Sussex* (1591).
Tilley	Morris Palmer Tilley, *A Dictionary of the Proverbs in England in the Sixteenth and Seventeenth Centuries* (Ann Arbor, MI, 1950).
Wilson	Jean Wilson, *Entertainments for Elizabeth I,* Studies in Elizabethan and Renaissance Culture II (Woodbridge, 1980).

INTRODUCTION: THE ROYAL PROGRESS

Though materials produced for the public stages of the early modern period have long formed part of the academic curriculum and are broadly familiar to the general reader, there remains little widespread understanding of the variety of entertainments devised by sixteenth- and early seventeenth-century theatre practitioners for other types of performance space, and the overlap that existed between staged events of seemingly disparate kinds. While the plays devised for the boy companies of the private playhouses and items written for academic audiences are currently attracting a greater degree of notice and beginning to find their way on to the twenty-first-century stage,[1] the numerous playlets performed in the course of the royal progress, for all the wealth of scholarship devoted to them,[2] remain largely unfamiliar to both students and the public at large. The recent publication of a revised edition of John Nichols's *The Progresses and Public Processions of Queen Elizabeth I*[3] has performed an invaluable service in making a substantial proportion of this vast body of material more widely available to those working in the field, but the cost of a five-volume set, the density of the presentation, and the old-spelling nature of the edition make the work inaccessible to all but a dedicated few.[4] The aim of the present volume, a fully annotated, modern-spelling edition of a small number of representative texts, is to promote a more widespread understanding of this area of late sixteenth-century dramatic activity, and thus to contribute to the growing contemporary awareness of the distorted view of Elizabeth culture effected by a divorce between materials produced for the public theatres, plays performed at the private playhouses, pageants mounted for civic occasions, and the shows devised for the amusement of the monarch in the course of her annual progress.

At first glance, the five entertainments included in this selection might suggest a highly exclusive type of diversion, far removed in terms of its content and the country-house seclusion of its setting from both the more familiar forms of Elizabethan theatrical activity and the day-to-day actualities of sixteenth-century life. All five, performed in the course of a visit by the sovereign to a prominent member of the social elite, are supremely non-naturalistic, exclusively directed to the monarch, and firmly located in the context of court panegyric. Paradoxically, however, they are representative of a genre that forms an integral part of a highly pragmatic project to strengthen the bond between ruler and ruled, in that like her present-day namesake, the current incumbent of the throne, Elizabeth I, firmly believed that the monarch needed to be seen in order to be believed. The annual progress that took place from one country house to another during the summer months for much of the reign, passing through towns and villages in the Midlands, and to the south, east, and west of the capital,[5] involved not only Elizabeth herself and numerous members of her court but much of the machinery of state, requiring extensive preparations on the part of her nominated hosts, civic authorities, and the populace through whose districts she passed. A record of the Queen's visit to Coventry in 1566, en route to the Kenilworth seat of the Earl of Leicester, for example, states that:

> The maior and aldermen of the citie of Coventrie, not havyng a monethes warnyng of her graces pleasure herein, endeuored them selues to provide all and sett in order all thynges within the citie, The hie waies wheyre her grace should passe were Repaired and amended, the gates of the citie paynted with her maiesties armes, the streites graveled, the houses and buyldinges Refreshed with sondrie colours, manie showes provided in sondrie places to staie her grace with all and generallie euery thing sett foorthe in as good order as tyme and space wold permitt.[6]

The participation of a considerable number of people would clearly have been required in the mending of the roads and refreshing of paintwork, and, though the task of welcoming the Queen to the city by means of an oration fell to the city Recorder, it was the guildsmen who mounted the 'showes' by which she was entertained as she passed with her train through the streets. Nichols records that 'The Tanners Pageant stood at St John's Church; the Drapers at the Cross; the Smiths at Little Park-street; and the Weavers at Much Park-street'.[7] While the Queen watched the shows devised for her entertainment, the populace were thus intimately involved in facilitating the much more magnificent spectacle afforded by the progress itself, at once actors in and observers of a protracted event explicitly designed to reinforce the power and prestige of the monarch in the consciousness of the community at large.[8]

The inhabitants of the various settlements through which the monarch progressed were not alone in reshaping their environment in response to their sovereign's presence. The vast numbers of people involved in the progress required considerable forethought and restructuring on the part of her prospective hosts, abruptly obliged to supply accommodation appropriate to every level of the royal entourage. The account of the Queen's visit to Elvetham, for example, includes an extensive list of numerous temporary buildings (many elaborately decorated) erected for the use of both the monarch herself and her attendants, together with catering facilities capable of furnishing dining tables some twenty-three yards in length, and a banquet of a thousand dishes served by two hundred staff (see *Elvetham*, lines 36–7 and 619–24).[9] On occasion, even the landscape itself was transformed in response to the monarch's arrival. At Elvetham, a large lake sufficient to accommodate three islands, a number of vessels, and a troupe of performers was constructed as a site for a number of spectacular events, including a stately parade of marine deities and a battle between sea gods and satyrs (see *Elvetham*, lines 45–61). A host of labourers, builders, and skilled craftsmen were thus involved in the preparations prior to the visit itself,[10] while an army of servants was needed to ensure the smooth running of the event.

The populace were not excluded, moreover, once the visit was under way, and neighbouring gentry were called upon to participate in what was essentially a community endeavour.[11] The author of the account of the entertainment at Elvetham notes that 'near ten thousand people' (line 109) were gathered to witness the monarch's ceremonial entrance to the park, while 'as Her Majesty sat at dinner, there was a door set wide open for air, whereby the people might (to their great comfort) behold Her Majesty's presence in open view' (lines 335–7). The proximity of unsophisticated spectators to the performance on the lake, and thus to the sovereign herself, is indicted by the observation that 'Sylvanus, being so ugly ... affrighted a number of the country people that they ran from him for fear, and thereby moved great laughter' (lines 524–6). Though it is doubtful that all of the ten thousand gathered to welcome their sovereign could hear much of the welcoming shows, or that those able to do so would understand the Latin oration, the impressive nature of the monarch's entourage, together with the use of a language associated with the Church, would have communicated something of the elevation of the monarch at work in the ceremonial nature of her reception, while the spectacular nature of the pageant on the lake would not have been lost on its wider audience, for all the naivety of their response. Local performers were called upon, moreover, on some occasions, to contribute to the entertainments themselves, and thus had some degree of ownership of what was essentially a courtly event. At Cowdray, for example, 'the country people presented themselves to Her Majesty in a pleasant dance with tabor and pipe, and the Lord Montague and his lady among them, to the great pleasure of all the beholders and the gentle applause of Her Majesty' (lines 270–4).

While the conditions of the royal progress brought a wide spectrum of the populace into contact with the monarch, the entertainments themselves, though remote from the capital in terms of the venues in which their performance took place, were far from divorced from the centres of cultural production in other respects. Aristocratic writers, London theatre playwrights, prominent academics, and noted musicians all contributed to a genre that brought high culture into a rural setting. Sir Philip Sidney wrote *The Lady of May* for the entertainment at Wanstead (1578); George Gascoyne (author of *Supposes*, an early verse comedy adapted from Ariosto's *Suppositi*) was a major contributor to the shows mounted in the course of the monarch's stay with the Earl of Leicester at Kenilworth (1575); John Lyly (the principal court dramatist of the 1580s) composed the Angler device for the Queen's visit to Chiswick (1602), and may also have contributed to the entertainment at Cowdray (1591);[12] Richard Mulcaster (headmaster of Merchant Taylors' School, and author of a pamphlet recording the pageantry attending the Queen's coronation) supplied Latin verses for the entertainment at Kenilworth, while William Hunnis (Master of the Children of the Chapel Royal) devised the welcoming speech for the same event. The Queen's own musicians performed for her during her visit to Cowdray (line 47 below), and at Elvetham (1591) she was delighted by a notable pavan, composed by Thomas Morley, organist at St Paul's, which she graced with a new name. Songs by prominent composers punctuate the texts. A piece by the erudite poet and dramatist Thomas Watson, for example, accompanied the Queen's entrance to Elvetham (lines 123–89), and songs by Nicholas Breton (lines 572ff.) and Edward Johnson (lines 681–90) among others weave their way through the events that ensued.[13] The Office of the Revels may well have provided the properties required for spectacular effects (e.g. the severing of the hubristic Ceres' harvest cart at Bisham), while contemporary literary works are directly quoted or evoked. An adaptation of a palindrome from Lyly's *The Woman in the Moon* (3.1.111–15), for example, is inscribed on an escutcheon presented to the monarch at Elvetham (see lines 512–15), and the title figure of Spenser's *The Faerie Queene* dances beneath Her Majesty's window in the course of the same visit. The visual arts are not excluded, moreover, from the eclectic sweep of the artistic scope. The tree bearing the arms of the gentlemen of Sussex, to which the Queen is conducted during her visit to Cowdray, constitutes a literalization of the pictorial representations of aristocratic relationships adorning the houses of members of the nobility (see line 112n.), while the deficiencies of contemporary murals, among other art works, find their way into the topical *paragone* debate which forms the principal subject of the surviving material from *Mitcham* (see lines 12–198).

Just as the entertainments performed in the course of the royal progress were informed by contemporary art forms, they in turn informed the centres of cultural life. Although descriptions of many visits were preserved only among private papers (e.g. *Mitcham* and *Chiswick*), detailed accounts of others were published, running in some instances through more than one edition (cf. the variant texts of *Cowdray* and *Elvetham* discussed on pp. 23–4 and 54). The appetite for access to the pastimes of the aristocratic elite, signalled by the growing late sixteenth-century market for play texts promoted by reference to their production at court,[14] brought material designed for provincial performance on to the bookstalls of the capital, enabling an urban readership to encounter an otherwise inaccessible genre, and allowing the transfer of material to other contexts and performance modes. The entertainment at Elvetham, for example, has been credited with influencing both Nashe's *Summer's Last Will and Testament* and Shakespeare's *A Midsummer Night's Dream*,[15] while versions of songs from, but not necessarily composed for, a number of entertainments appeared in the verse miscellany *England's Helicon* (1600),[16] with their performance during a royal progress explicitly noted on some occasions (see *Bisham*, line 132.1n.).

Though composed for a range of venues over a protracted period of time, the country-house entertainments performed in the course of Elizabeth's reign, typified by those in this volume, conform in large measure to a pattern, and may thus be described as a distinct genre. The monarch is commonly met on her arrival at the entrance to the house, or (more usually) the park, by a figure associated with the creative arts, either by occupation (cf. the Poet at Elvetham) or through his or her evocation of a literary mode, most commonly the pastoral or piscatorial tradition (cf. the Angler at Chiswick). The terms of the encounter serve to initiate the sovereign's entrance into a non-naturalistic environment peopled by classical deities, shepherds and shepherdesses, anglers, dairymaids, and wild men of the woods, a world where Ovidian transformations may be effected, and the physical actualities of time and place are translated into a timeless never-never-land, superficially remote from the everyday world. The speaker is frequently dismayed at the rustic inadequacy of the accommodation afforded by the residence of the prospective host (cf. the Dairymaid's insistence at Harefield that her master's home is 'but a Pigeon-house',[17] and the Angler's concern at Chiswick at the prospect of the Queen lodging in an unfinished 'shed' (line 3)). The monarch herself is cast, not as a passive spectator in the encounter, but as an active participant in the fiction, occupying a liminal position between audience and actor in the ensuing playlet or show. At Cowdray, for example, it is her arrival, the Porter informs us, that brings his vigil to an end, undoing by her entrance a curse under which the castle has lain, and endorsing the fidelity of her host through her acceptance of a key. At Bisham her arrival tames the Wild Man of the woods, who learns civility as a result of her presence; at Mitcham she accepts a petition presented by a messenger on his master's behalf; while at Chiswick she takes a pen from an Angler, in order to sign a pardon for the inadequacies of the 'unrepaired cottage' (line 18) in which she will be obliged to lodge.

As the visit progresses, she is drawn more fully into a series of fictions turning on her participation, transforming the entire country house and its environment through her presence into a stage. As she moves towards the house at Elvetham, for example, the Graces and Hours remove blocks placed by Envy in her path, a spectacle made meaningful only by her advance; in a playlet at Kenilworth, the goddess Diana recognizes her as her lost nymph Zabeta, and marvels at the impressive figure that she has become; at Bisham, an encounter with Ceres causes the latter to recognize the emptiness of her self-glorifying claims; while at Wanstead she determines the outcome of *The Lady of May* in deciding which of her two suitors the title figure will accept. Music of a variety of kinds contributes to the ethereality of the world that the speakers and quasi-mythical events combine to evoke, while the presentation of rich gifts, woven into the fabric of the diversions, draws further creative processes into the range of art forms invoked. At Bisham, for example, the crown of wheat ears which Ceres lays in a gesture of deference at the monarch's feet is ornamented with a jewel (cf. the jewel she receives from Nereus at Elvetham); at Harefield, St Swithin presents her with a rainbow robe he has taken from Iris; while at Mitcham the Poet, Painter, and Musician offer her an embroidered gown, having recognized the limitations of their own arts in failing to capture her worth.

The terms in which the sovereign is addressed in the course of her visits are also important in relation to both the artistic strategies at work in the construction of the entertainments and the larger purposes of the progress itself. The names under which she is celebrated in Elizabethan panegyric (e.g. Eliza, Cynthia, Diana) constantly recur, inviting association with both contemporary poetic effusions (e.g. the April Eclogue of Spenser's *The Shepheardes Calender*) and the plays produced by juvenile troupes for performance at court (e.g. Lyly's *Endymion*). While implying the virtues for which she was celebrated (e.g. chastity and constancy), her association with mythological figures and classical deities denotes a quasi-divine state, her capacity to transform the lives of her subjects, her glory, power, and prestige, contributing to that mystification of the monarchy at work throughout Elizabeth's reign, designed to reinforce an initially questionable right to the throne. Recurrent motifs (e.g. familiar classical stories, and courtly debate topoi turning on the virtues of the sovereign) contribute, moreover, to the consistent projection of a transcendent state. The fable of Philemon and Baucis, for example, is repeatedly called upon to mirror the immeasurable social distance between all-powerful beneficent monarch and humble well-meaning host (cf. *Elvetham*, lines 206–7, and *Bisham*, lines 109–10); while both the propriety and impossibility of seeking to represent, or pay adequate tribute to, the supreme excellence of the ruler is repeatedly debated (cf. *Mitcham, passim*). The latter motif implicitly endorses the state's rigid control of the Queen's image – intended to impress her supreme unchanging regality on the public mind – a strategy which, like the progress itself, played a significant part in Elizabethan propaganda.[18]

Though superficially no more than fanciful trivia far removed from the dangerous undercurrents of sixteenth-century public life, the progress entertainments may thus be described as broadly political in intent, in that they contributed to the promotion of the cult of the Virgin Queen, and its dissemination beyond the social elite. The progress also served more immediate state purposes, however, reflected in part in the choice of aristocratic houses that the monarch elected to visit. Though her stays with royal favourites (e.g. the Earl of Leicester at Kenilworth) and old friends (e.g. Lady Russell at Bisham) are unsurprising, and some manors were patently chosen on the grounds of convenience in the course of extended journeys, other visits were clearly projected with very different considerations in mind. The most extensive item in this selection (*The Entertainment at Elvetham*), for example, records a lengthy visit to the Earl of Hertford, whose career had not exemplified that unswerving loyalty to the Crown that might seem to warrant the honour of hosting the sovereign (see p. 47), while in choosing to stay at Cowdray the Queen was pointedly electing to reside with a prominent adherent of the Catholic faith, at a time when the attempted invasion of England by the Spanish Armada was still fresh in the public mind (see p. 18) and a further foray from across the channel remained a continuing threat. In such instances, the warmth of her reception, from the extensive preparations, through the earnest expressions of admiration, and effusive celebrations of her beauty, to the lavish banquets, valuable gifts and flattering attention to her personal tastes, may be interpreted not simply as straightforward exhibitions of devotion to the sovereign devoid of any deeper intent, but as highly charged coded conversations between insecure hosts and a distrustful guest – a means of asserting unqualified loyalty and thus potentially cementing an uncertain relationship in some cases,[19] and functioning as a measure of fidelity for the monarch in others, confirming suspicions of disaffection or enabling an expression of trust.[20]

Visits to friends and known adherents were not free, moreover, from that jockeying for social position and pursuit of personal advancement characteristic of the Elizabethan court. The *Princely Pleasures* at

Kenilworth, the most celebrated and extensive of all the entertainments devised for the monarch in the course of her progress, is widely regarded, in Jean Wilson's words as 'Leicester's final throw in the marriage-game which he had been playing [with Elizabeth] for the first sixteen years of the reign',[21] a game in which Sidney's *Lady of May,* performed three years later at Wanstead (see p. 4), may also have played a significant part.[22] Among the items in this collection, the hope of courtly preferment is implicit in the pastoral playlet devised to welcome the monarch to Bisham, a piece plainly designed to showcase the talents of the hostess's daughters (by whom it was performed) in the hope of commending them to the monarch's attention (see pp. 94–5). The swift publication of a number of entertainments immediately after the visit took place (cf. *Cowdray* and *Elvetham*) represented a further means, moreover, of self-promotion, exhibiting the affluence, social prominence, and good taste of the host, while, for those further removed from court circles, it was the hope of securing the financial benefits flowing from royal patronage, as Sir Julius Caesar's private papers make clear, that justified the vast sums they were obliged to disburse in meeting the exacting requirements of a monarchical stay (see pp. 110–11).

Though the royal progress took place for much of the reign, the five items included in this edition are all drawn from the period 1591–1602, and a number of considerations governed the decision to limit the selection to material produced at that time. Many of the entertainments mounted in previous decades survive in fragmentary form alone, or are merely noted in court records or private papers among other aspects of the progress itself. The two most outstanding examples of the genre prior to 1591, the entertainments at Wanstead and Kenilworth, are currently available, in whole or part, in a variety of modern-spelling editions readily available to the student or general reader,[23] and the sheer scale of the latter militates against its inclusion in a volume designed to exhibit the consistency and range of the genre as a whole.[24] By contrast, the texts of a substantial number of pieces survive from the later years of the reign, affording a variety of perspectives on the relationship between the progress entertainments and other late Elizabethan forms of artistic expression, and validating their discussion as a coherent body of work relevant to a number of twenty-first-century disciplines and critical concerns. Unlike the entertainments at Kenilworth and Wanstead, moreover, none of the items in this selection, for all their interest for a twenty-first-century reader, has previously appeared in a fully annotated, modern-spelling edition based on all the surviving accounts, four of the five having been published only in lightly annotated old-spelling editions, while the history of the fifth, *The Entertainment at Elvetham*, has been dogged by editorial confusion consequent on the loss of the second quarto (see pp. 54–5). It is not solely the relative neglect of the majority of the pieces by recent editors, however, that determined their inclusion in this edition. The five items have been chosen with a view to exhibiting both the consistent features of the genre and the diversity of insights afforded by progress entertainments into a range of aspects of late Elizabethan cultural life – the tensions surrounding the position of the Catholic nobility (*Cowdray*), the lavish expenditure and extensive preparations entailed in hosting the monarch (*Elvetham*), the avenues of expression available to aristocratic women (*Bisham*), the embeddedness of this group of diversions in pan-European cultural discourse (*Mitcham*), and the invaluable biographical information to be garnered from a seemingly marginal early seventeenth-century text (*Chiswick*).[25]

It is the collaborative nature of the progress entertainments, however, exhibited by the items in this edition, which is perhaps the most illuminating aspect of a type of diversion seemingly remote from the core achievements of the contemporary Elizabethan stage. Whereas the works designed for the public and private playhouses of the early modern period were once exclusively discussed in terms of the products of particular creative minds, divorced from the contexts in which they were initially performed, it is now widely recognized that the plays that have come down to us, even those ascribable to a single hand, are the product of a collaborative endeavour on the part of playwrights, promoters, censors, actors, musicians, stage designers, copyists, and printers.[26] Similarly, a wide range of talents is drawn on in the texts presented below, from the writers who devised the playlets, through the learned composers of the Latin orations, the musicians and song writers responsible for the musical interludes, the costume and set designers tasked with realizing the often highly spectacular effects, the jewellers who produced the gifts worthy of presentation to the sovereign, the actors and dancers, pyrotechnicians, workers in sugar, huntsmen and sportsmen who brought the projected amusements to fruition, to those who, in some instances, gathered the material together for the press.[27] Rather than being divorced from the cultural life of the wider community by virtue of their episodic nature and the *ad hoc* character of the locations in which they were performed, the entertainments may thus be seen as symptomatic of the process of play-making in the Elizabethan age, and the richness of the theatrical culture from which the canonical plays of the early modern period emerged.

As the items in this collection exhibit, however, the entertainments designed for the royal progress differ from the products of the public playhouses of the early modern era in one major respect. Whereas the performers who entertained the audiences of the capital were exclusively male, the principal actor in the progress entertainments was a woman, in that the monarch herself functioned as both the focus of attention and an active participant in the Arcadian world created for her amusement. It is she who, in the person of the 'the wisest, the fairest, and most fortunate of all creatures' (lines 14–15), brings stability to the castle walls at Cowdray; she who, in the person of Cynthia, causes Ceres' chariot at Bisham to split; she who, as 'a sea-born Queen' (line 535) at Elvetham, bestows an auspicious name on Neaera's barque; she who enters into the fiction at Mitcham to receive a bejewelled gown; and she who at Chiswick exhibits her graciousness in signing a pardon with the Angler's pen.[28] Above all, it is her presence, and the impromptu responses that she is called upon to make, that endow every aspect of the entertainments staged for and around her with meaning. The shows presented in the course of the royal progress suggest, in short, that the most distinguished actor on the early modern stage was not Burbage, Alleyn, Armin, or Kempe but the sovereign herself.

A NOTE ON THE TEXTS

The most difficult decision taken in the preparation of this volume has been the mode of referencing to adopt, in that the five items included in the selection have survived in documents of a variety of kinds.[29] Two (*Cowdray* and *Elvetham*) have come down to us in more than one early modern printed edition, the texts of which vary between their initial and subsequent publication, and include both factual information and performance-related accounts. One, *Bisham*, was published soon after the progress took place, but only the welcoming playlets (performed in the course of the monarch's progress towards the house) are preserved in the collection in which the entertainment appeared, and nothing more has survived from the remainder of the visit. Two items, *Mitcham* and *Chiswick*, survive in manuscript form alone, and remained unpublished until 1953 when they appeared together in an old-spelling edition. The former includes both spoken and sung material, together with the contents of a document undisclosed to the audience at large, while the latter consists of only two speeches, one delivered on the Queen's arrival, and the other on her departure from the house.

The diverse nature of the documents in which the materials have come down to us would seem, at first sight, to preclude a uniform approach to the editing of the texts. While some (e.g. *Mitcham* and *Chiswick*) invite presentation in accordance with the conventions of The Revels Plays, in that they consist of speeches and stage directions alone, others (i.e.

Cowdray and *Elvetham*) cannot be accommodated within the procedures governing the presentation of play texts, in that the dramatic material is interwoven with substantial descriptive passages, relating not merely to aspects of performance but to the circumstances of the visit itself, and necessitating (in some cases) the inclusion of extensive alternative readings. In order to impose some degree of consistency on the collection, it was therefore decided to follow the procedures adopted in *Masques of Difference* (ed. Kristen McDermott, Revels Student Editions, 2007), a collection of items by Ben Jonson posing similar problems in their inclusion of descriptive material (including matters of staging), dialogue, and song. In line with McDermott's edition, through line numbering has been employed throughout, with all material derived from the copy text (including stage directions and circumstances of performance) included in the count, but with modern editorial interventions (e.g. interpolated stage directions designed to clarify the work for the twenty-first-century reader) unnumbered, and signalled, in accordance with Revels conventions, by square brackets.

The decisions taken in response to the problems presented by the several items in the collection are set out, in each case, in a prefatory note, and amplified, where necessary, in the collation. It is hoped that a uniform approach to the referencing of the texts will be seen as preferable to an awkward dislocation between those in which through line numbering has been necessitated by the nature of the copy text and others seemingly inviting the use of more familiar Revels conventions.

FURTHER READING

The monumental *The Progresses and Public Processions of Queen Elizabeth I*, initially published by John Nichols between 1788 and 1823, and recently revised, under the general editorship of Elizabeth Goldring, Faith Eales, Elizabeth Clarke, and Jayne Elisabeth Archer, with the assistance of a team of over fifty scholars (5 vols, Oxford University Press, 2014), constitutes the obligatory starting point for all those engaged in the study of any aspect of the Elizabethan progress. The edition includes all extant materials known to Nichols relating to the planning of, and preparations for, the progress itself, together with the devices performed for the monarch during her visits to private estates, documents pertaining to relevant political events, civic welcomes, and other kinds of entertainments (e.g. tournaments and emblematic 'shows') mounted for the sovereign in the course of her reign. The concluding volume includes an extensive bibliography, comprising both primary (pre-1700) printed sources and modern editorial and critical works, together with a helpful biographical dictionary designed to assist the reader in identifying individuals prominent in the records but now largely unknown.

The scale of the bibliography (over 125 pages) is indicative of the degree of interest that this body of material has attracted in recent years, and the prioritization of any particular field in the present survey would inevitably invite the charge of an unwarranted neglect of other, equally illuminating, areas of scholarly investigation. For this reason, all material relating to textual transmission (a major concern with this group of texts) is dealt with in separate prefatory notes to each of the pieces edited below, enabling this summary to deal with historical and interpretative criticism alone. A useful starting point for the navigation of the field is supplied by a collection of essays, *The Progresses, Pageants, and Entertainments of Queen Elizabeth I* (Oxford, 2007), edited by Jane Elisabeth Archer, Elizabeth Goldring, and Sarah Knight, all of whom formed part of the editorial team responsible for the revision of Nichols's work cited above. As Mary Hill Cole points out in the opening remarks to her contribution, 'Thanks to John Nichols ... our approach to progresses has developed in almost as many directions as he provided documents' ('Monarchy in Motion: An Overview of Elizabethan Progresses', pp. 27–45, p. 27), and the themes explored in the essays that follow amply justify that contention. The topics addressed in the course of the volume range from gift-giving ceremonies (Felicity Heal, 'Giving and Receiving on Royal Progress', pp. 46–61), through the purposes and spectacular nature of university visits (Siobhan Keenan, 'Spectator and Spectacle: Royal Entertainments at the Universities in the 1560s', pp. 86–103), the interplay between politics and religion in an East Anglian progress (Patrick Collinson, 'Pulling the Strings: Religion and Politics in the progress of 1578', pp. 122–41), to the circulation of manuscript copies of the texts of the entertainments themselves (Gabriel Heaton, 'Elizabethan Entertainments in Manuscript: The Harefield Festivities (1602) and the Dynamics of Exchange', pp. 227–44). Of particular interest in relation to the items in the present edition are Elizabeth Heale's discussion of the politico/religious purposes of *The Entertainment at Cowdray* ('Contesting Terms: Loyal Catholicism and Lord Montague's Entertainment at Cowdray, 1591', pp. 189–206), and Peter Davidson and Jane Stevenson's essay on female authorship in the early modern period ('Elizabeth I's Reception at Bisham (1592): Elite Women as Writers and Devisers', pp. 207–26), both of which turn on topics considered in relation to the pieces edited here.

For all the broad sweep of the essays noted above, none is concerned with that most crucial aspect of sixteenth-century royal entertainments – the music that accompanied every species of monarchical diversion. It is this aspect of court culture in the later sixteenth century which is explored in Katherine Butler's *Music in Elizabethan Court Politics* (Woodbridge, 2015), an invaluable study of the significance of the music performed for the sovereign both in private (i.e. by members of her own household) and in the wider public arena. The section dealing with 'Politics, Petition, and Complaint on the Royal Progress' (pp. 143–91) is particularly relevant to the present edition, but the close relationship between the progress entertainments and music-infused royal occasions of a variety of kinds make the book as a whole pertinent to an understanding of the nuances of a culturally remote body of material difficult of access on the printed page.

Equally helpful in enabling the contextualization of the work is David Bergeron's magisterial survey of early modern civic pageantry, *English Civic Pageantry 1558–1642* (London, 1971, rev. ed. Tempe, AZ, 2003). Though the focus of the work is broader than the progress entertainments themselves, it nevertheless supplies an insight into the wide range of pageants and processional materials of which the country house entertainments form part, exhibiting their embeddedness in the sixteenth-century social landscape, as opposed to the cultural void that they appear to occupy to the modern reader, attuned to the conditions governing the production of the canonical works of the Elizabethan–Jacobean stage.

More directly relevant to the pieces in this selection is Jean Wilson's *Entertainments for Elizabeth I* (Woodbridge, 1980). The volume includes unnumbered, old-spelling editions of four entertainments – *The Four Foster Children of Desire* (1581), *Cowdray* (1591), *Elvetham* (1591), and *Ditchley* (1592), the first of which falls outside the scope of the present volume, while the text of the third is unreliable (as is the accompanying site map) in that the edition was produced before the rediscovery of the second quarto. The relegation of the notes to the back of the volume also constitutes a major disadvantage for modern readers attempting to get to grips with an unfamiliar body of work. For all its limitations, however, the volume is worthy of note, in that the texts are prefaced by a substantial introduction, including old-spelling editions of two further entertainments, those at Bisham and Rycote (1592), together with a discussion of the historical circumstances from which the entertainments emerged, and a variety of facets of the cult of Elizabeth that developed around the monarch in the course of the reign.

Further removed from all but one of the entertainments in this edition, but similarly illuminating in terms of their cultural context, is Chloe Porter's *Making and Unmaking in Early Modern English Drama* (Manchester, 2013), a study of a sixteenth-century aesthetic rooted in the notion of incompletion (i.e. works of art as an ongoing process, rather than as 'finished' compositions). The fragmentary nature of the progress pieces, consisting in large measure of interludes or episodic encounters, devoid of any point of closure other than some compliment to or acceptance by the monarch, serves to align them with other examples of the aesthetic explored in Porter's work, and with the purposes for which that concept was employed. An understanding of the aesthetic is particularly helpful in relation to the *Entertainment at Mitcham*, in which the notion of incompletion is brought into play in a discussion of the impossibility of depicting the superlative character of the monarch, furnishing a link with other examples of court panegyric in which a similar device is employed (see p. 112 below).

The multidisciplinary nature of the approach required for research into this area of creative activity is exemplified in an essay by H. Neville Davies ('Looking Again at Elvetham: An Elizabethan Entertainment Revisited', in Margaret Shewring and Linda Briggs, eds, *Waterborne Pageants and Festivities in the Renaissance*, Farnham, 2013), tracing his investigation into the chequered history of *The Entertainment at Elvetham*. In arriving at an accurate edition of the work and a reliable reproduction of its site map, Davies explores the historical circumstances surrounding the visit for which it was devised, the publication of the first and second editions, the history of the progressive corruption of the text following the loss of the second quarto, the successive distortions of the site map, the topography determining the actual location of the principal components of the performance, the erroneous assumptions of its literary editors, culminating in the mistaken belief in the existence of a third early edition, the trail of evidence leading to the rediscovery of the second quarto, the reconciliation of textual and physical evidence enabling reliable historical and literary discussion, and the 'rich texture of interwoven conceits' (p. 233) an understanding of which is required for its decoding. The essay stands as both a model and a warning for all those seeking to venture into this field, exhibiting the daunting reality that no contribution to the study of civic and country house entertainments can ever be anything other than work in progress.

NOTES

1 The Read Not Dead series of rehearsed readings of non-canonical works, directed by James Wallace under the auspices of Globe Education, and the performance of plays designed for early modern juvenile troupes by a company of boy actors from the King Edward VI School, Stratford, under the direction of Perry Mills, have proved particularly influential in this respect. Notable productions by the latter include Lyly's *Galatea* at the Sam Wanamaker Theatre in 2014 and Beaumont's *The Woman Hater* at The Other Place and King's College Chapel (London) in 2016.

INTRODUCTION: THE ROYAL PROGRESS 15

2 A comprehensive bibliography of the relevant material may be found in Elizabeth Goldring, Faith Eales, Elizabeth Clarke, and Jayne Elisabeth Archer, gen. eds, *John Nichols's The Progresses and Public Processions of Queen Elizabeth I*, 5 vols (Oxford, 2014), v, pp. 398–526. All subsequent references to Nichols's work are to this edition.
3 For full bibliographical details see previous note.
4 The decision not to include material discovered subsequent to the publication of Nichols's work (e.g. the entertainments at Mitcham (1598) and Chiswick (1602)) has also limited the value of the project.
5 The progress travelled through Kent, for example, in 1573, to Bristol in 1574, to Worcester in 1575, and through Norfolk and Suffolk in 1578.
6 Quoted from *Nichols*, i, pp. 453–4. Compare the account of the much more extensive preparations for the beautification of the city at Norwich prior to the Queen's visit to the city in 1578 (*Nichols*, ii, pp. 779–84).
7 See Gabriel Heaton (ed.), *Nichols*, i, p. 452 and n.
8 For a fuller account of the scale of the preparations required prior to the progress, the substantial costs involved, and the anxieties of the prospective hosts, see Chambers, i, pp. 108ff.
9 Similarly the dining table at Cowdray was twenty-four yards long (line 185), while the forethought required prior to the Queen's visit to Theobalds in 1583 is indicated by a document detailing the numerous rooms needed for members of the royal train, from the grooms of the privy chamber, through officers of the cellar and pantry, the clerk of the kitchen, to the gentlemen ushers and the nobility themselves (see *Nichols*, iii, pp. 186ff.).
10 At Elvetham, we are told, 'two hundred or thereabouts' artificers were required for the construction of new buildings alone (line 15).
11 Chambers notes, for example, in relation to the Queen's visit to Harefield in 1602, that 'Sir Thomas Egerton's friends came nobly to his assistance, and sent in innumerable presents, including no less than eighty-six stags and bucks, eleven oxen, sixty-five sheep, and forty-one sugar-loaves, as well as birds, fish, oysters, Selsea cockles, cheese-cakes, sweetmeats, wine, wheat and salt' (i, p. 118).
12 For a detailed discussion of the Lyly's role in the production of material for the royal progress, see Leah Scragg, 'Angling for Answers: Looking for Lyly in the 1590s', *Review of English Studies*, NS 67/279 (2015), pp. 237–49 (Advance Access, 18/11/2015).
13 For a more detailed account of the authorship of the musical components of the Elvetham entertainment, see H. Neville Davies, in *Nichols*, iii, pp. 568–9.
14 See Andy Kesson, *John Lyly and Early Modern Authorship*, Revels Plays Companion Library (Manchester University Press, 2014), pp. 138ff.
15 Its influence may also have extended to Purcell's *The Fairy Queen*, see H. Neville Davies, '"To Sing and Revel in these Woods": Purcell's *The Fairy-Queen* and *The Honourable Entertainment at Elvetham*', *Renaissance Journal* 1/6 (June 2002), *passim*.
16 Elizabeth Goldring notes, for example, that the collection 'contains fourteen poems by Sidney, including a brief extract from the Wanstead entertainment' (*Nichols*, ii, p. 543).
17 Quoted from Bond, i, p. 492, lines 7–8.
18 For a fascinating account of state control of the sovereign's image during the Elizabethan period, see Roy Strong, 'Depicting Gloriana', in Donald Stump and Susan M. Felch, eds, *Elizabeth I and Her Age*, Norton Critical Editions (New York and London, 2009), pp. 746–69, reprinted from *Gloriana: The Portraits of Elizabeth I*

(London, 1987), pp. 9–45. The emphasis on the impossibility of representing the monarch also serves to align the work with other literary modes and popular sixteenth-century works (e.g. Lyly's *Euphues and His England*, pp. 332–3).

19 Cf. the Queen's comment to Hertford on her departure from Elvetham, discussed on pp. 53–4 below.

20 See the Queen's assurance to Montague at Cowdray (lines 36–7), discussed on pp. 19–20 below.

21 *Entertainments for Elizabeth I* (Woodbridge, 1980), p. 22.

22 Arthur F. Kinney, for example, describes the work as 'as much propaganda as pageant' (p. 37).

23 The *Entertainment at Kenilworth*, for example, is included in *Elizabeth I and Her Age* cited in n. 18 above (pp. 195ff.), while the *Lady of May* appears in Kinney's anthology (pp. 38ff.).

24 The same problem arises with the similarly extensive entertainment at Woodstock (1575), from which a selection would not do justice to the scale and complexity of the piece.

25 See the introductions to the relevant entertainments for detailed discussions of the topics summarized here.

26 For a revealing example of the number of possible contributors to the production of an early modern play text, see *The Booke of Sir Thomas More* (BL MS Harley 7368). A lithographic reprint of the manuscript, ed. W.W. Greg, was published by The Malone Society in 1911 and revised in 1961 by F.P. Wilson and Arthur Brown with additional critical material by Harold Jenkins.

27 A collected edition of a number of entertainments was published by Joseph Barnes, for example, in 1592.

28 A number of plays presented at court similarly place the sovereign in a liminal position as both audience to and actor in a fictional event (e.g. Peele's *The Judgement of Paris*), while other forms of royal entertainment (e.g. tournaments and tilts) are frequently evocative of an all-embracing theatrical milieu. A description of the arrangements for the tournament for the Duc de Montmorency noted, for example, that 'those that beheld [the effect]deemed it rather a Theater celestiall, then a pallace of earthly building', while the participants in the event are described as 'Actors' (quoted from *Nichols*, ii, p. 21).

29 Full bibliographical details may be found in the introductory material prefacing each of the items below.

THE ENTERTAINMENT AT COWDRAY

INTRODUCTION

Of all the visits undertaken by Elizabeth I in the course of her summer progress, her week-long stay with Anthony Browne, Viscount Montague, at Cowdray (14-20 August 1591) was among the most politically charged. Though Montague, a lifelong supporter of the Tudor monarchy, had entertained Edward VI, the Queen's brother, in 1552, and occupied a series of significant positions in the course of her sister's reign,[1] in the fraught atmosphere following the Babington plot of 1586,[2] the resultant execution of Mary Queen of Scots in 1587, and the attempted Spanish invasion of 1588, he was regarded with considerable suspicion by the Elizabethan regime, in that he was a known adherent of the Catholic faith.[3] In a speech delivered to a group of friends in 1592, Montague himself remarked, that 'yt hath bene tolde her maiestie ... that yt was dawngerous commynge for her to my house', that he harboured 'syx score recusantes', and was 'a dawngerous man to the state'.[4] It is clear, nevertheless, that the monarch herself was determined on the visit, whatever the reservations of her court. In a letter to Sir William More in July 1591, alerting him to a projected stay by the Queen, Lord Hunsdon noted that, 'her Maiesty is resolued to make a progresse this yeare as far as Portsmouth, and to begin the same the 22 or 23 of this month, and to come to your house. She is verie desyrous to go by Petworth and Cowdry, yf yt be possible.'[5]

The Queen's decision to undertake the visit to Cowdray was not based on any uncertainty regarding the religious convictions of her prospective host. Rather than seeking to dissimulate his beliefs, Montague made no attempt to conceal his devotion to the old religion, though he was adamant that his Catholicism was not synonymous with disloyalty to the state.[6] Addressing members of his circle in the year following the Queen's visit, for example, he declared that:

> I am a Catholyque in my religeon which I keepe to my selff; I seeke to drawe no man to that religeon, neather chylde nor servant, but let them doo theyr conscyences therein ... [But] yf I shoulde knowe that anye of youe my bretheren or children shoulde concent unto anye suche thinge, as to ioyne with Pope or forreyne potentate, I woulde be he that should fyrst present youe or anye of youe to the Quene and her Cowncell.[7]

The terms of the assertion indicate that many of his acquaintance shared his religious, if not his political, beliefs, and the friends and kinsmen gathered around him for the monarch's visit might well have been judged a threat to the security of the realm through a potential division between their social and spiritual obligations (see lines 282–5n.). The visit was consequently conducted against a background of insecurity on the one hand and suspicion on the other, encapsulated in the delicate interplay between loyalty and mistrust played out in the sequence of thematically related entertainments mounted for the monarch in the course of her stay.

In common with the majority of progress entertainments, the shows presented at Cowdray usher the spectator into a non-naturalistic universe, inhabited by figures drawn from a range of literary genres involved in some species of flattering interaction with the Queen (see pp. 5–7). Rather than simply turning on some form of tribute to the sovereign, however, the Cowdray entertainments are bound together through the exploration of a single motif, the problematic nature of the subject/monarch relationship at a time of religious and political unrest. The show that greeted the Queen's arrival, for example, clearly looks back to the most celebrated of the entertainments devised in the course of Elizabeth's reign, the festivities at Kenilworth in 1575, but the thrust of the device is very different from that of the interlude from which it derives. As at Kenilworth, the monarch is met on her arrival by a Porter equipped with a club and the castle keys, who is moved by her supreme virtue to surrender the insignia of his office into her care. Whereas the Porter at Kenilworth is initially enraged, however, by the unaccustomed activity in the forecourt of the castle, only to be 'perced at the prezens of a parsonage so euidently expressing an heroicall Soueraintie ouer all the hole estates',[8] at Cowdray the encounter is woven into a myth denoting the uncertain relationship between monarch and host. The Porter recounts a prophecy stating that the castle roof would 'totter' (line 14) until the entrance of 'the wisest, the fairest, and most fortunate of all creatures' (lines 14–15), and indicates that his fellow porters, despairing of its fulfilment, had fallen asleep and had been turned into posts, and would consequently fail to witness the new stability that her arrival ensured. The entry of the monarch thus becomes symbolic of the security that the expression of trust signalled by the visit affords her host, while the presentation of the castle key denotes the open access that he is ready to afford her to his innermost self. The show concludes, moreover, with a direct affirmation of the mutual confidence that the arrival of the monarch confirms, with the Porter asserting that 'in duty and service to Your Majesty [his master] would be second to none' (lines 32–3), and the Queen declaring in answer that 'she would swear for him there was none more faithful' (lines 36–7). The tensions surrounding the visit, and the consequent relief of the onlookers at the positive nature of the exchange, may be measured by the emotional reaction of the lady of the house, who, we are told, 'as it were weeping in [the Queen's] bosom' exclaimed 'Oh happy time! Oh joyful day' (lines 39–40).

The theme was sustained in the entertainment provided for the following Monday, which took the form of a hunt,[9] for which the Queen was presented with a crossbow, to the accompaniment of a song.[10] Like the Porter's speech, the lyric turns upon the nature of the bond between ruler and ruled, but appropriates analogies, in this instance, conventionally associated with contemporary amatory effusions (e.g. 'Behold her locks like wires of beaten gold': line 53). The imagery serves to situate the relationship in the context of courtly love (a conventional strategy in Elizabethan panegyric), and the closing lines draw together the specific occasion of the performance (i.e. the projected hunt) and the perilous nature of the lover's, and hence the subject's, situation:

> Your eyes are arrows though they seem to smile,
> Which never glanced but galled the stateliest hart.
> Strike one, strike all, for none at all can fly,
> They gaze you in the face although they die.
> (lines 67–70)

The predicament defined in the passage (unswerving devotion accompanied by fear of the dangers attendant upon loss of favour) is presented here in highly personal terms, in striking contrast to the strategy employed in the quasi-dramatic entertainment performed on the following day, which widens the focus of the governing interest from the position of the individual (i.e. that of Montague himself) to a more broadly based 'display of regional loyalty',[11] locating the stance of the Catholic household at Cowdray within a deep-rooted commitment to the service of the monarch embracing the county of Sussex as a whole.

Having been 'bountifully feasted' (lines 78–9) at the Priory, to which her host had withdrawn for the duration of her stay, Elizabeth is met in the gardens by a Pilgrim, who relates a bruising encounter with a Wild Man, who denies him access to an oak tree hung with shields, and an equally uncomfortable meeting with a virago, who claims her name is Peace, but who vociferously bars his path. The encounter serves to position the Queen as a chivalric figure, petitioned for succour by a complainant in need of redress, and the chivalric mode is sustained in the interlude that ensues. Having been conducted to the tree in question, which proves to be hung with 'Her Majesty's arms, and all the arms of the noblemen and gentlemen of that shire … in escutcheons most beautiful' (lines 111–12), Elizabeth is addressed by the Wild Man (an embodiment of ancient, rural England), who explains to her that the tree and its escutcheons, which he and Peace so vigorously defend, represent the county, united in its devotion to her service, and that the roots of the oak are so deeply rooted 'that Treachery, though she undermine to the centre, cannot find the windings' (lines 132–3). The highly resonant notion in the 1590s of a strategic coastal community united in the defence of the realm against both invasion and subversion runs throughout the speech, culminating in an assertion that contrives to present the conduct of the monarch and the stance of the tree's owner as an exemplum of an ideal behavioural relationship that ensures the security of both subject and state:

> Abroad, courage hath made you feared; at home honoured clemency. Clemency which the owner of this grove hath tasted in such sort that his thoughts are become his heart's labyrinth, surprised with joy and loyalty – joy without measure, loyalty without end – living in no other air than that which breathes Your Majesty's safety. (lines 140–5)

While sustaining the emphasis on loyalty, the closing lines of the Wild Man's speech broaden the focus of the unifying theme still further, moving beyond both the individual and the county to a direct reflection on the condition of the times. The hostility directed by the Wild Man and Peace towards the Pilgrim, conventionally an unthreatening figure regarded with respect, is attributed to a pervasive duplicity in social and religious spheres that both generates and justifies mistrust. Hence the Pilgrim is a figure of suspicion, because in a world in which all men 'practise what they should not' (line 157) a seemingly harmless, worthy individual may constitute a threat, since 'one can scarce know a pilgrim from a priest' (lines 154–5). The opposition between 'pilgrim' and 'priest' here is a significant one, given the Catholic associations of the latter term and its emphatic repudiation by proponents of extreme Protestant thought.[12] Its use in a negative context and association with social unrest imply that a devout adherence to the old religion was not to be equated with approval of the wave of disguised Catholic clergy then seeking to enter the country as the subversive agents of foreign powers – a highly meaningful implication given the religious affiliations of the group gathered at the foot of the tree.[13]

The 'ditty' which immediately follows the Queen's encounter with the Wild Man serves, however, to qualify the affirmation of enduring loyalty with which the previous interlude draws to a close, in that it ends on an intimation that even the most deep-seated devotion may ultimately wither through rejection and neglect (cf. 'Love, Fancy's birth, Fidelity the womb, / The nurse Delight, Ingratitude the tomb': lines 178–9). While being general in application, the admonition may have had its origins in Montague's removal from the Privy Council following the Queen's accession to the throne, and the loss of his position as Lord Lieutenant of the County in the course of the 1580s.[14] Though couched in discreet terms, the purport of the song (that unswerving loyalty is deserving of reward) would not have been lost on a monarch long accustomed to coded advice from members of her court,[15] and the 'winding of a cornet' and 'most excellent cry of hounds' (line 180) by which the piece was immediately succeeded may well have been designed to forestall prolonged (and potentially adverse) reflection on the warning by means of a change of mood.

The following day's entertainment co-opted yet another literary mode to the central motif. Walking in the gardens in the evening, the Queen was brought to a fishpond where an Angler, as if unaware of her presence, reflected on the degenerate condition of the times. The device, which belongs to the piscatory tradition (a minor branch of the pastoral mode), differs in its conduct from the previous shows, in that it situates the monarch in the position of an observer rather than an active participant in the scene, and she is not overtly implicated in the action until directly addressed by a Netter at the close (though the brightness of her presence does allow the fish to evade the Angler's hook). The Angler's occupation, involving luring fish to their destruction by means of a deceptive bait, is used as a metaphor for a universal tendency to deceive and entrap, extending from the deceptive practices of merchants and landlords, through manipulative private behaviour, to the disingenuous conduct of some members of the social elite. The Angler's reflections clearly constitute a development of the Wild Man's notion of a 'disguised world' in which 'one can scarce know a pilgrim from a priest' (lines 154–5), and the political aspect of the theme is developed in the exchanges that ensue. On being joined by a Netter, the Angler ceases to be the focus of attention, while the Netter reflects on the subject of disloyalty, asserting his own devotion to the monarch and his hostility to those who are never satisfied 'till they have disturbed the state with their treacheries' (lines 237–8).

Like the two previous shows, the interlude concludes with a love song, couched in this instance in terms of the fishermen's occupation, rather than the behaviour of mythical creatures or the language of courtly love. Though the enduring nature of the lover's devotion is repeatedly asserted (cf. 'Our habits base, but hearts as true as steel': line 256), reciprocity is seen, once again, as fundamental to the relationship (cf. the conditional nature of the assertion 'Love me, and I'll love thee': line 259), while a lack of responsiveness is represented in negative terms by means of a pun (cf. 'We count them lumps that will not bite at love': line 265). The song concludes with the Netter laying his catch at the monarch's feet, transforming the customary presentation of a valuable gift (cf. *Elvetham*, lines 407–13, and *Mitcham*, lines 210–12) into a symbolic enactment of the proposition that 'Whatsoever there is, if it be good, it is all yours' (lines 245–6). Like the previous shows, the interlude as a whole was patently designed to be read by the monarch as bearing on the doubts relating to Montague's position, with the Netter's emphatic repudiation of those seeking to disturb the status quo, together with his wish that 'all the hollow hearts to Your Majesty were in my net' (line 232), constituting a further assurance of his fidelity, and of his readiness to surrender disloyal members of his acquaintance to the justice of the Elizabethan state.[16]

The evening entertainment on the last full day of the visit enacted, by means of a 'pleasant dance' (line 271), an ideal version of the social relationships explored in the course of the stay. The event was performed by 'the country people' (lines 270–1), to the accompaniment of unsophisticated instruments appropriate to their social class (cf. 'tabor and pipe': line 272), but Lord and Lady Montague were also among the dancers. Their presence served to extend the tribute to the monarch from the common people to the social group as a whole, presenting an image of a patterned society, its members moving in harmony with one another, from the music-loving sovereign for whom the entertainment was designed, through the nobility, to the humblest members of the realm.

The monarch's response to the sustained insinuations of the entertainments took the form of an ancient ceremony performed the following day. Prior to her departure, the Queen knighted six of those present during her visit, four of them close members of Montague's family circle, and all but one known (or suspected) to be adherents of the Catholic faith (see lines 280–1 and 282–5n. below). The ceremony constituted a significant gesture of trust by the monarch in those of her nobles dissenting from the established Church, simultaneously cementing their loyalty, and justifying the prosecution of the visit as a mechanism for confirming (and rewarding) the fidelity of both a dissident community and the prominent members of a county crucial to the defence of the realm.

The closing lines of the account of the visit ('So departed Her Majesty to the dining place, whither the Lord Montague and his sons, and the Sheriff of the Shire, attended with a goodly company of gentlemen, brought Her Highness': lines 286–8) are indicative in their social inclusiveness of its success, and the paradigm of fidelity and reward that it enacted was swiftly communicated to the public at large. Within weeks of the Queen's departure, an account of the visit was printed by Thomas Scarlet for the publisher William Wright, and the interest that it generated may be measured by the fact that a second edition was published before the end of the year. The two editions, variously entitled *The Honorable Entertainment Giuen to the Queenes Maiestie in Progresse, at Cowdrey in Sussex* (hereafter *Hent*) and *The Speeches and Honorable*

Entertainment giuen to the Queenes Maiestie in Progresse, at Cowdrey in Sussex (hereafter *Shent*), differ in a number of respects, and the order in which they were published remains a matter of dispute.[17] While *Hent* (STC 3907.5 / BL C.142.dd.23) describes the events of the visit in greater detail (most notably those of the last two days, entirely omitted by *Shent*), *Shent* (STC 3907.7 / BL C.33.d.11), includes three songs, which do not appear in *Hent*,[18] suggesting that they were recovered subsequent to the initial publication of work, and that *Shent* is thus the later edition.[19] Whatever the order of their publication, and their deficiencies as a record of the visit as a whole, the two texts afforded the reading public a significant insight into an event which bore directly on contemporary anxieties but from which they were physically and socially removed, and the fact that the second, at least, was compiled by a spectator concerned to stress the political importance of the relationship between monarch and host[20] suggests that their publication was prompted, not by their literary distinction but by a desire to bolster Montague's position and to offer a measure of reassurance to the more moderate members of the Catholic community as a whole.[21]

For all their topical interest, however, neither edition of the entertainments mounted at Cowdray afforded the urban reader an insight into the lavish nature of the spectacles engineered for the monarch's amusement at some of the estates that she visited in the course of her progress (e.g. at Kenilworth in 1575), or of the army of participants occasionally required for their execution (see *Elvetham*, p. 3). The performative aspects of the entertainment follow a simple repetitive pattern of a formal speech (or speeches) followed by a song on a related theme, and only three actors were needed for the execution of the various roles – a Porter on the Queen's arrival, a nymph to present her with a crossbow, a Pilgrim to encounter her in the gardens, a Wild Man to explain the barring of the Pilgrim's passage to the tree, and an Angler and a Netter to meet her by the fishpond – no more than two of whom needed to be present at the same time. Instrumentalists and a singer (who may have doubled as the nymph) were also required, but were supplied from the Queen's own musicians (see lines 45–7), while country people were enlisted for the performance of a dance. Settings and stage properties were similarly sparse. All the encounters took place in the open air, within or at the entrance to the park. Two posts, carved to represent porters, were sufficient to furnish the initial encounter on the bridge, while the Porter himself was equipped with a club and keys. A bower was needed for the nymph in which to present the Queen with the crossbow prior to the hunt, and painted escutcheons were required for the oak tree guarded by the Wild Man. There is no evidence to suggest that the fishpond, needed for the closing device, was specifically dug for the occasion (in contrast to the site of the sea battle at Elvetham), and a fishing rod, a net, and some real or artificial fish were all the stage properties that the encounter with the two fishermen required. Costuming was confined to the provision of armour for the Porter, garments appropriate to a mythical being for the nymph, a russet-coloured velvet coat with a matching hat, the latter decorated with cloth of silver scallop shells, for the Pilgrim, garments of ivy for the Wild Man, and fishing gear for the Angler and the Netter. In short, the experience afforded by the entertainment to both primary and secondary audiences was primarily verbal rather than visual, designed to promote reflection on contemporary political issues rather than wonder or surprise, with a perception of the lavish expenditure traditionally associated with the monarch's progress confined for the reader to a brief mention of 'the proportion of breakfast' on the Sunday of the visit amounting to 'three oxen and one hundred and forty geese' (line 43), and of the Queen being 'feasted most sumptuously' the following Wednesday, 'at a table four-and-twenty yards long' (lines 184–5).

The authorship of the shows performed in the course of the entertainment, like the order in which the two editions were published, remains a matter of dispute. The material is not ascribed to a writer by a contemporary witness of any kind, or specified in the early editions, though it was later attributed to John Lyly by R. Warwick Bond, in his collected edition of the dramatist's work, on the grounds that it echoes the Lylian canon at a number of points.[22] Though Bond's attribution was discounted in 1962 by G.K. Hunter in his groundbreaking study of Lyly's work,[23] and receives little notice in Gabriel Heaton's edition in the revised *Nichols*,[24] the case for Lyly's authorship has been recently revived, and it is now evident that it rests upon much firmer ground than was previously supposed.[25] The discovery of the entertainment at Chiswick, ascribed to Lyly in a contemporary hand (see p. 132 below), confirms that he was still engaged in the production of entertainments for the monarch long after he had ceased to write for the stage, and the fact that *Cowdray* and *Chiswick* are the only two extant progress entertainments to feature an Angler forges a significant link between the two works. The echoes detected by Bond (detailed in the notes to the present edition) span the entirety of the Lylian corpus, embracing not only his published and unpublished plays but the prose works on which his reputation was initially built, together with his contribution to the Martin Marprelate debate, written only two years before the Cowdray entertainment was composed. Analogies used throughout the Lylian canon carry the same connotations, moreover, as elsewhere in Lyly's work (e.g. the association of the drinking habits of camels with treachery and dissention),[26] implying a degree of familiarity with the corpus in its entirety hard to attribute to any writer other than Lyly himself. The choice of Lyly as deviser may have been suggested, moreover, by the antagonism to extreme Protestant thought evidenced by his contribution to the Martin Marprelate debate, while his experience as writer of highly sophisticated court entertainments may have commended him to a host anxious both to please and articulate a position. In the absence of further documentary evidence, however, the most that currently can be said regarding the conception of the work is that Lyly is a strong contender for the authorship of the angling device at least, and that he may well have been influential in the composition of the entertainment as a whole.

A NOTE ON THE TEXT

While both 1591 texts of the Cowdray entertainment offered a contemporary reader a degree of insight into the conduct of the event, neither constitutes an adequate basis for a twenty-first-century edition, in that both are plainly defective as a record of the occasion as a whole. As noted above (p. 24), none of the songs performed in the course of the visit is recorded by *Hent*, while *Shent* omits much of the narrative material supplied by *Hent*. For that reason, the present edition, like its old spelling predecessors,[27] presents a conflated text, substantially based on *Hent*, but incorporating the additional material supplied by *Shent*, with points of variance between the two editions recorded in the notes. Given the disparate nature of the material supplied by the two witnesses (narrative, direct speech, dramatic interludes, songs), through line numbering has been utilized throughout, in common with the rest of the items in this volume, both to aid ease of reference and to promote understanding of the easy flow between types of entertainment and from one entertainment to another characteristic of the genre as a whole. It is hoped that the continuity implied by the numbering system, together with the sense of familiarity arising from the use of use of modern spelling, punctuation, and printing conventions, will help to diminish the distance between the twenty-first-century reader and a species of event remote from the modern world, facilitating entry into a universe in which Arcadian figures talk politics to a mythologized sixteenth-century Queen.

NOTES

1 Created Viscount Montague in 1554, he was elected to the Garter and became a member of the Privy Council in 1555, and was a commander of the English forces at St Quentin in 1557 (see Gabriel Heaton, *Nichols*, iii, p. 550).

2 Designed to reinstate Catholicism in England through the assassination of Elizabeth and the installation of Mary Queen of Scots on the English throne, the plot was detected by Walsingham's network of spies, leading to the execution of Mary herself.
3 Contemporary suspicions regarding the ultimate loyalties of the Catholic gentry during this period were not without foundation. Aristocratic houses (including Cowdray) were known to shelter continental priests, while the commanders of English forces on the continent surrendered the garrisons at Zutphen and Deventer to the Spanish in 1587, prior to the attempted Spanish invasion of England.
4 Quoted from Heaton, *Nichols*, iii, p. 550.
5 Quoted from Jayne Elisabeth Archer (ed.), *Nichols*, iii, p. 547.
6 For an illuminating discussion of contested notions of the relationship between political and religious affiliations in the late sixteenth century, and their application to the *Entertainment at Cowdray*, see Elizabeth Heale, 'Contesting Terms: Loyal Catholicism and Lord Montague's Entertainment at Cowdray', in *Progresses*, pp. 189–206.
7 Quoted from Heaton, *Nichols*, iii, p. 551.
8 Quoted from Elizabeth Goldring (ed.), *Nichols*, ii, p. 244.
9 A popular aristocratic pastime (cf. *LLL*, 4.1. *passim*).
10 For a detailed exploration of the political implications of the musical elements of the entertainments performed in the course of the royal progress, see Butler. *The Entertainment at Cowdray* is discussed on pp. 165–70.
11 Wilson, p. 52.
12 See, for example, the 'Epistle', in Joseph L. Black, ed., *The Martin Marprelate Tracts* (Cambridge, 2008), pp. 25 and 224 n. 127.
13 A rather different interpretation of the Queen's encounter with the Pilgrim is offered by Elizabeth Heale, who suggests that the contrast between the stance of the monarch towards the Pilgrim and the aggression of those who bar his passage to the tree, 'both of whom are unable to distinguish the pilgrim's innocent motives from those of an enemy', is designed to differentiate between 'Elizabeth's discerning mildness' and the 'misjudging belligerence of her government, its officers, and its anti-Catholic propaganda' (*Progresses*, p. 200).
14 See Butler, p. 168.
15 The monarch's remarkable facility in deciphering coded materials is borne out by a letter from William Cecil to his son, in which he remarks, regarding an allegorical epistle: 'Never a lady beside her, nor a decipherer in the court, would have dissolved the figure to have found the sense as her Majesty hath done' (quoted from Butler, p. 170n.).
16 Once again, Elizabeth Heale offers a rather different interpretation of the encounter, equating the fisherman with adherents of the Catholic faith (cf. St Paul as a 'fisher of men'), and those who are never satisfied until they have 'disturbed the state with their treacheries' (lines 237–8) with 'the real traitors, the ... immoral exploiters who operate unchecked within the Protestant state' (*Progresses*, p. 203).
17 For a fuller discussion of the discrepancies between the texts and the probable order of their publication, see Heaton (*Nichols*, iii, pp. 548–9).
18 The omission of sung material from play texts is not uncommon during the period and may derive from the fact that songs were not regarded as an integral part of the dramatic text but were held separately by their composers or performers (see G.K. Hunter, *John Lyly: The Humanist as Courtier* (London, 1962), pp. 367–8). The majority of Lyly's plays, for example, initially published in the 1590s, did not

include the songs until 1632, when they were recovered by Edward Blount for his collected edition, while it has been calculated that over thirty songs are missing from Massinger's plays.
19 The contrary argument is advanced by Butler, who argues that 'The edition including the lyrics may have been prepared prior to the progress to be given out as a guide to events, while the version without was published afterwards' (p. 166).
20 Cf. 'And so her Maiestie well pleased with her welcome, & he throughly comforted with her Highnesse gracious acceptance, shee went from thence': collation, lines 266–91n.).
21 Though there is no record of the further publication of either of the two editions, there is some faint indication that the entertainment continued to attract interest. In 1598 the bookseller William Barley was punished for having sold a copy for 2d, and, though the circumstances of the offence are entirely unclear, it is evident that some market existed for the text. Of the three songs, the first two stanzas of the first were included by Robert Jones in his collection *The Muses' Garden for Delights* in 1610, though the omission of the final verse, which is specific to its performance at Cowdray, suggests that by the time of its publication in the collection its topical relevance was no longer of interest.
22 See Bond, i, pp. 404–9.
23 John Lyly, p. 84.
24 See *Nichols*, iii, pp. 549–50.
25 See Leah Scragg, 'Angling for Answers: Looking for Lyly in the 1590s', *Review of English Studies*, NS 67/279 (2015), pp. 237–49.
26 Cf. *Euphues and His England*, p. 282, *Mother Bombie*, 5.3.253–5, *Pap with an Hatchet*, 'Indifferent Reader', lines 15–16.
27 By Bond (1902), for example, Wilson (1980), and Heaton in the revised *Nichols* (2014).

THE ENTERTAINMENT AT COWDRAY

AUGUST 14

The Queen, having dined at Farnham, came with a great train to the right honourable the Lord Montague's on Saturday, being the 14th day of August, about eight of the clock at night. Where, upon sight of Her Majesty, loud music sounded, which at her entrance on the bridge suddenly ceased. Then was a speech delivered by a personage in armour, standing between two porters carved out of wood, he resembling the third, holding his club in one hand and a key of gold in the other, as followeth.

SATURDAY

THE PORTER'S SPEECH [TO HER MAJESTY]

The walls of Thebes were raised by music, by music these are kept from falling. It was a prophecy since the first stone was laid that these walls should shake and the roof totter till the wisest, the fairest, and most fortunate of all creatures should, by her first step, make the foundation stayed, and by the glance of her eyes make the turret steady. I have been here a porter many years. Many ladies have entered passing amiable, many very wise, none so happy.

---

1. 14] *Shent*; 18 *Hent*. [For the variant versions of the text see pp. 23–4.] 2. The Queen ... Farnham] *Hent*; The Queens Maiesty *Shent*. 3. on] *Hent*; upon *Shent*. 14th] This ed.; 14 *Shent*; 15 *Hent*. 11.] Bracketed material this ed.

---

2. *Farnham*] Surrey residence of Thomas Cooper (Bishop of Winchester).
3. *Lord Montague's*] Cowdray Park in West Sussex, home of Anthony Browne, 1st Viscount Montague (title variously recorded as Montagu and Montecute).
5. *sounded*] was played.
6–33. *Then was ... to any*] Compare the giant Porter at Kenilworth, equally forbidding in appearance, who yields his keys to the monarch in recognition of her outstanding worth (*Nichols*, ii, pp. 244–5).
7. *porters*] gatekeepers.
12. *The walls ... by music*] The stones of which the walls of Thebes were constructed were reputed to have moved themselves into place at the sound of the music played by Amphion on his lyre. The myth is alluded to by Lyly in *Campaspe* (1.1.39–40).
16. *stayed*] firm.
18. *passing amiable*] exceedingly beautiful.
happy] fortunate.

These my fellow porters, thinking there could be none so noble, fell on sleep, and so incurred the second curse of the prophecy, which is never again to awake. Mark how they look more like posts than porters, retaining only their shapes but deprived of their senses. I thought rather to cut off my eyelids than to wink till I saw the end. And now it is: for the music is at an end, this house immovable, your virtue immortal. O miracle of Time, Nature's glory, Fortune's empress, The World's wonder! – Soft. This is the Poet's part, and not the Porter's. I have nothing to present but the crest of mine office, this key. Enter, possess all, to whom the heavens have vouchsafed all. As for the owner of this house (mine honourable lord), his tongue is the key of his heart, and his heart the lock of his soul. Therefore what he speaks you may constantly believe, which is that in duty and service to Your Majesty he would be second to none, in praying for your happiness equal to any.

> *Tuus O Regina quod optes*
> *Explorare fauor; huic iussa capessere fas est.*

Wherewithal Her Highness took the key and said she would swear for him there was none more faithful. Then, being alighted, she embraced the Lady Montague and the Lady Dormer, her daughter. The mistress of the house (as it were weeping in her bosom) said, 'Oh happy time! Oh joyful day!'

---

19. so noble] *Hent*; such *Shent*. 26. Fortune's empress] *Shent*; Fortune: Empresse *Hent*. 36–43. Wherewithal ... forty geese] *Hent*; not in *Shent*.

---

20. *second curse ... prophecy*] The curse under which the house was reputed to labour was held to have run its course in 1797, with the extinction of the title (following the death of the 9th Viscount) and the destruction of the castle, four years earlier, by fire.

23. *wink*] close my eyes, blink.

27. *part*] role. The terms in which the monarch is celebrated here are, in fact, repeated in the 'Ditty' (i.e. the 'Poet's part') at lines 57–8.

28. *crest*] badge.

29. *vouchsafed*] given, entrusted.

30–1. *his tongue ... soul*] i.e. his tongue opens up his heart, and his heart allows access to his soul.

34–5. *Tuus O ... fas est*] 'Your task, O Queen, is to search out your desire; my duty is to do your bidding.' The lines derive from Virgil's *Aeneid* (I, 76–7), where they are spoken by Aeolus to Juno, Queen of the gods.

36–7. *she would swear ... faithful*] a significant assertion given Montague's known Catholicism (see pp. 18–19).

38. *the Lady Dormer*] Elizabeth, wife of Robert Dormer of Wing in Buckinghamshire. Her husband was among those knighted at the close of the Queen's visit (see lines 280–5). Her brother, Sir Anthony Browne (Montague's eldest son), was married to her husband's sister, Mary.

THE ENTERTAINMENT AT COWDRAY   31

That night Her Majesty took her rest, and so in like manner the next day (which was Sunday), being most royally feasted. The proportion of breakfast was three oxen and one hundred and forty geese.

MONDAY

On Monday at eight of the clock in the morning Her Highness took horse with all her train and rode into the park, where was a delicate bower prepared, under the which were Her Highness' musicians placed, and a crossbow by a nymph, with a sweet song, delivered to her hands to shoot at the deer (about some thirty in number), put into a paddock; of which number she killed three or four, and the Countess of Kildare one.

A DITTY

Behold her locks like wires of beaten gold,
Her eyes like stars that twinkle in the sky,
Her heavenly face, not framed of earthly mould,
Her voice that sounds Apollo's melody,
The miracle of Time, the world's story,
Fortune's Queen, Love's treasure, Nature's glory!

No flattering hope she likes, blind Fortune's bait,
Nor shadows of delight, fond Fancy's glass,
Nor charms that do enchant, false Art's deceit,
Nor fading joys, which Time makes swiftly pass,

---

47. *were Her ... placed*] *Hent*; were placed her Highnes Musitians *Shent*.   48–51. *and a crossbow ... one*] *Hent*; and this dittie following song while her Maiestie shot at the Deere *Shent*.   52–70. A DITTY ... *they die.*] *Shent*; not in *Hent*.

42–3. *proportion of*] amount supplied at.
43. *three oxen ... geese*] There is some evidence to suggest that the lavish provisions required in the course of a royal visit (cf. *Elvetham*, lines 619–49) did not always depend solely on the resources of the host, but might be supplemented by friends or the neighbouring gentry (see Chambers, i, p. 118, and p. 3 n. 11 above).
46. *train*] attendants.
47. *Her Highness' musicians*] As Wilson notes (p. 158 n. 13), the phrasing suggests that this element of the entertainment was supplied by the court musicians rather than members of Lord Montague's household. The text gives no indication whether it was a member of this troupe who performed the 'ditty' sung at lines 52ff. below.
50. *Countess of Kildare*] Either the then Countess, Frances Fitzgerald, daughter of Charles Howard, 2nd Baron Howard of Effingham, who performed the dubbing ceremony recorded at lines 277–85, or the dowager Countess, Lord Montague's sister.
53. *like wires ... gold*] a commonplace simile, ridiculed in Shakespeare's sonnet 130.
56. *sounds Apollo's melody*] i.e. is as melodious as the music of Apollo.
60. *fond*] foolish.

> But chaste desires which beateth all these down,
> A goddess' look is worth a monarch's crown.
>
> Goddess and monarch of this happy isle, 65
> Vouchsafe this bow, which is an huntress' part.
> Your eyes are arrows though they seem to smile,
> Which never glanced but galled the stateliest hart.
> Strike one, strike all, for none at all can fly,
> They gaze you in the face although they die. 70

Then rode Her Grace to Cowdray to dinner, and about six of the clock in the evening, from a turret, saw sixteen bucks, all having fair law, pulled down with greyhounds in a lawn. All the hunting ordered by Master Henry Browne, the Lord Montague's third son, ranger of Windsor forest. 75

TUESDAY

On Tuesday Her Majesty went to dinner to the Priory, where my lord himself kept house, and there was she and her lords most bountifully feasted.

After dinner, she came to view my lord's walks, where she was met 80 by a Pilgrim, clad in a coat of russet velvet fashioned to his calling, his

---

73–5. All the hunting ... forest.] Hent; *not in* Shent. 80–3. After dinner ... following.] Hent; *not in* Shent.

---

64. *A goddess' look*] Having the aspect of a goddess.
66. *vouchsafe*] deign to accept.
an huntress' part] (a) appropriate to a huntress; (b) an attribute of Diana, chaste goddess of the hunt (with whom Elizabeth was frequently associated in Elizabethan panegyric).
68. *galled*] wounded.
hart] male deer after its fourth year (with a pun on 'hart'/'heart').
69. *none at ... fly*] It was contrary to etiquette to turn one's back on the monarch, enabling the implied equation between deer and the Queen's courtiers in the closing lines.
72–3. *fair law*] a good start.
73. *lawn*] stretch of grassy untilled ground.
74–5. *ranger ... forest*] officer entrusted with the overall operations of Windsor forest (now known as Windsor Great Park). The office was traditionally held by one close to the monarch (currently Prince Philip).
77. *dinner*] midday meal, usually eaten around twelve o'clock (cf. *Elvetham*, line 331n.).
the Priory] Eastbourne Priory, where the Earl himself lodged during the Queen's visit (hence *where my lord himself kept house*: lines 77–8). The Priory had formed part of the Cowdray estates since 1536.
80. *my lord's walks*] probably Closewalks Wood, to the south of Cowdray, as Heaton notes (*Nichols*, iii, p. 554 n. 119), an area of woodland laid out in walks and enclosed with yews.
81. *fashioned ... calling*] designed in accordance with his occupation.

hat being of the same, with scallop shells of cloth of silver, who delivered her a speech in this sort following.

THE PILGRIM'S SPEECH

Fairest of all creatures, vouchsafe to hear a prayer of a pilgrim, 85
which shall be short, and the petition, which is but reasonable. God
grant the world may end with your life, and your life more happy
than any in the world. That is my prayer. I have travelled many
countries, and in all countries desire antiquities. In this island, but
a span in respect of the world, and in this shire, but a finger in 90
regard of your realm, I have heard great cause of wonder, some
of complaint. Hard by, and so near as Your Majesty shall almost
pass by, I saw an oak, whose stateliness nailed mine eyes to the
branches and the ornaments beguiled my thoughts with astonishment. I thought it free, being in the field, but I found it not so. 95
For, at the very entry, I met I know not with what rough-hewed
ruffian, whose arms were carved out of knotty box, for I could
receive nothing of him but boxes. So hasty was he to strike, he
had no leisure to speak. I thought there were more ways to the
wood than one, and finding another passage I found also a lady, 100
very fair but passing froward, whose words set me in greater heat
than the blows. I asked her name. She said it was Peace. I wondered that Peace could never hold her peace. I cannot persuade
myself since that time but that there is a wasps' nest in mine ears.
I returned discontent. But if it will please Your Highness to view 105

---

84. THE PILGRIM'S SPEECH] *Shent*; Pilgrime *Hent*.

---

82. *scallop shells*] Originally designating one who had undertaken a pilgrimage to the shrine of St James at Compostela in Spain, the scallop shell had evolved into a generalized emblem of a pilgrim by the mid-sixteenth century.
    cloth of silver] high-status material interwoven with fine threads of silver.
86–8. *God grant ... world*] Compare the similarly brief closing prayer at Bisham, wishing that the Queen's 'days may increase in happiness, [her] happiness have no end, till there be no more days' (lines 167–8).
89. *desire antiquities*] seek for historical artefacts.
90. *span*] maximum distance between the tip of the little finger and the thumb, used as a measure of length (= 9 inches).
92. *Hard by*] Near here.
95. *free*] of open access.
96. *rough-hewed*] unpolished, uncultivated in manners and appearance.
97. *box*] high-density, close-grained wood used for fine carving.
98. *boxes*] blows (cf. modern 'boxing').
99–100. *more ways ... one*] appropriate proverbial expression (Tilley, W179), signifying the availability of more than one option.
100. *passage*] route.
100–1. *a lady ... froward*] The same formulation occurs in Lyly's *Midas* at 3.3.32–3 (*passing froward* = exceedingly contentious).
103. *hold her peace*] be quiet.

it, that rude champion at your fair feet will lay down his foul head, and at your beck that lady will make her mouth her tongue's mew. Happily Your Majesty shall find some content; I more antiquities.

Then did the Pilgrim conduct Her Highness to an oak not far off, whereon Her Majesty's arms, and all the arms of the noblemen and gentlemen of that shire, were hanged in escutcheons most beautiful; and a Wild Man, clad in ivy, at the sight of Her Highness spake as followeth.

THE WILD MAN'S SPEECH AT THE TREE

Mighty Princess, whose happiness is attended by the heavens and whose government is wondered at upon the earth, vouchsafe to hear why this passage is kept and this oak honoured. The whole world is drawn in a map, the heavens in a globe, and this shire shrunk in a tree. That what Your Majesty hath often heard of with some comfort, you may now behold with full content. This oak, from whose body so many arms do spread, and out of whose arms so many fingers spring, resembles in part your strength and happiness, strength in the number and the honour, happiness in the

---

106. *that rude champion*] i.e. the wild man.
107. *beck*] gestured command.
107–8. *her tongue's mew*] a cage for her tongue (image derived from the confining (i.e. mewing) of birds of prey during the moult). The same image occurs in Lyly's *Mother Bombie* (cf. 'Mew thy tongue, or we'll cut it out': 2.1.127).
109. *antiquities*] ancient objects.
111. *arms*] armorial bearings.
112. *escutcheons*] shields. As Heaton notes, 'Painted trees hung with escutcheons representing counties were a decorative feature in a number of Elizabethan houses: a frieze in the great chamber at Gilling Castle included the arms of 433 Yorkshire families, and the green gallery at Theobalds was painted with fifty-two trees representing the English counties, each bearing the arms of the principal families of the county' (*Nichols*, iii, p. 556 n. 125).
113. *Wild Man*] embodiment of nature in its uncultivated state, evoking the 'green man', or 'wild man of the woods' of popular tradition. Compare the Wild Man who encounters the Queen in *Bisham*, lines 1–22.
115. *attended*] watched over.
116. *vouchsafe*] condescend.
117. *kept*] guarded.
118–19. *this shire ... tree*] See line 112n. above (*shrunk* = contracted into the form of).
122–3. *happiness*] good fortune.

truth and consent. All hearts of oak, than which nothing surer, nothing sounder; all woven in one root, than which nothing more constant, nothing more natural. The wall of this shire is the sea, strong but rampired with true hearts invincible. Where every private man's eye is a beacon to discover, every nobleman's power a bulwark to defend. Here [*He gestured to the tree.*] they are all differing somewhat in degrees, not duty, the greatness of the branches, not the greenness. Your Majesty may account the oak the tree of Jupiter, whose root is so deeply fastened that Treachery, though she undermine to the centre, cannot find the windings, and whose top is so highly reared that Envy, though she shoot on cop height, cannot reach her, under whose arms they have both shade and shelter. Well wot they that your enemies' lightnings are but flashes, and their thunder, which fills the whole world with a noise of conquest, shall end with a soft shower of retreat. Be then as confident in your steps as Caesar was in his fortune – his proceedings but of conceit, yours of virtue. Abroad, courage hath made you feared; at home honoured clemency. Clemency which the

---

129. SD] *This ed.*

124. *consent*] unity of mind.
hearts of oak] possibly the earliest recorded metaphorical use of the phrase (glossed in the phrase 'nothing surers nothing sounder' which follows).
surer] more reliable.
125. *sounder*] more loyal, truer.
126. *constant*] steadfast.
127. *rampired*] fortified.
128. *beacon to discover*] image denoting readiness to detect danger drawn from the use of beacons to alert communities to the threat of invasion. The lines that follow constitute an extended metaphor turning on the defeat of the Armada in 1588, and the continuing threat to the Elizabethan state from infiltration by enemy agents.
130. *degrees*] rank.
130-1. *the greatness ... branches*] i.e. the extent of their power and connections.
131. *greenness*] vigour.
account] consider.
132. *tree of Jupiter*] The oak was sacred to Jupiter (king of the gods) in Roman mythology.
134-5. *on cop height*] to the highest extent (*cop* = summit).
136. *Well wot they*] They know very well.
136-8. *enemies' lightnings ... retreat*] an allusion to the literal storm that frustrated the metaphorical storm threatened to the English state by the might of the Spanish Armada.
139-40. *his proceedings ... virtue*] Caesar's conduct motivated solely by a private persuasion, yours by virtue.
141. *honoured clemency*] mercy has made you honoured.
141-2. *Clemency ... such sort*] an allusion to the Queen's tolerance of Montague's known allegiance to the Roman Catholic faith, in contrast to her predecessors' treatment of those at variance with their own religious position (*in such sort* = to such a degree).

owner of this grove hath tasted in such sort that his thoughts are become his heart's labyrinth, surprised with joy and loyalty – joy without measure, loyalty without end – living in no other air than that which breathes Your Majesty's safety.

For himself, and all these honourable lords and gentlemen whose shields Your Majesty doth here behold, I can say this. That as the veins are dispersed through all the body, yet when the heart feeleth any extreme passion send all their blood to the heart for comfort, so they, being in divers places, when Your Majesty shall but stand in fear of any danger, will bring their bodies, their purses, their souls to Your Highness, being their heart, their head, and their sovereign. This passage is kept strait, and the Pilgrim, I fear, hath complained, but such a disguised world it is that one can scarce know a pilgrim from a priest, a tailor from a gentleman, nor a man from a woman. Every man, seeming to be that which they are not, only do practise what they should not. The heavens guide you, Your Majesty governs us. Though our peace be envied by them, yet we hope it shall be eternal.

Elizabetha deus nobis haec otia fecit.

---

156. man²] *Hent;* one *Shent.*   158–9. envied by them, yet] *Hent;* enuied, by you *Shent.*

142–4. *his thoughts ... end*] i.e. he is lost in a state of mingled happiness and devotion as a result of the unexpected clemency of the monarch's behaviour towards him.

144–5. *living in ... safety*] his life wholly committed to the safety of the Queen.

150. *divers*] a variety of.

153. *passage is kept strait*] route (to the tree) is closely guarded.

154. *a disguised world it is*] a reference to both the constant threat to the Elizabethan state from disguised agents of foreign powers, and the concealed purposes of those at home seemingly loyal to the throne.

155. *a pilgrim from a priest*] The distinction is an important one, in view of Montague's known Catholicism and reputed readiness to harbour priests.

a tailor ... gentleman] a reference to the sumptuary laws in force in the sixteenth century, dictating the type of materials to be worn by each social class and enabling rank to be perceptible at a glance.

156. *a man from a woman*] The comment turns on the supposition that the social functions of men and women are clearly defined and that gender roles should not be breached.

157. *practise*] (*a*) perform; (*b*) engage in plotting.

160. Elizabetha ... fecit] 'The god Elizabeth created this peace for us.' The line is adapted from Virgil (*Eclogues*, I, 6) where it reads 'O Meliboee, deus nobis haec otia fecit' ('O Melibeus, it is a god who gave us this peace').

THE ENTERTAINMENT AT COWDRAY

THE DITTY

There is a bird that builds her nest with spice,
   And built, the sun to ashes doth her burn,
Out of whose cinders doth another rise,
   And she by scorching beams to dust doth turn,   165
Thus life a death and death a life doth prove,
   The rarest thing on earth, except my love.

My love, that makes his nest with high desires,
   And is by beauty's blaze to ashes brought,
Out of the which do break out greater fires,   170
   They, quenched by disdain, consume to nought.
And out of nought my clearest love doth rise,
   True love is often slain, but never dies.

True love, which springs though Fortune on it tread,
   As camomile by pressing down doth grow,   175
Or as the palm that higher rears his head,
   When men great burdens on the branches throw.
Love, Fancy's birth, Fidelity the womb,
   The nurse Delight, Ingratitude the tomb.

Then, upon the winding of a cornet, was a most excellent cry of hounds,   180
and three bucks killed by the buck-hounds. And so went all back to
Cowdray to supper.

161–79. THE DITTY ... the tomb.] *Shent; not in Hent.* 181–2. and three ...
supper] *Hent;* with whome her Maiestie hunted and had good sport *Shent.*

---

   161. THE DITTY] The text gives no indication regarding the identity of the singer,
though the use of 'Then' at the start of the following paragraph implies that the piece
was performed between the encounter with the Wild Man and the pursuit of the buck
by the hounds.
   162–79] For a political reading of the ditty, see pp. 21–2.
   162. *There is ... spice*] the phoenix, reputed to construct a nest of spice on reaching
a certain age, and then to burn itself to ashes, before rising invigorated from the ruins
of its nest. The legend has an obvious application to Elizabeth (whose enduring beauty
was a recurrent theme of sixteenth-century verse) and to Montague's devotion to her
(figured in the singer's undying love).
   166. *prove*] show itself to be.
   174–7. *which springs ... branches throw*] Though both images are proverbial (Tilley,
C34 and P37), their proximity here and in Lyly's *Anatomy of Wit* (pp. 43 and 39) may
be significant in terms of the authorship of the entertainment (see pp. 25–6 above, and
lines 199–201n.).
   180. *winding*] sounding. For *cornet* see *Elvetham*, line 364n.
   cry] pack.
   182. *supper*] evening meal, taken between 5.00 and 8.00 pm.

WEDNESDAY

On Wednesday, the lords and ladies dined in the walks, feasted most sumptuously at a table four-and-twenty yards long. 185

In the evening Her Majesty, coming to take the pleasure of the walks, was delighted with most delicate music, and brought to a goodly fish pond, where was an Angler that, taking no notice of Her Majesty, spake as followeth.

THE ANGLER'S SPEECH 190

Next rowing in a western barge, well fare angling! I have been here this two hours and cannot catch an oyster! It may be for lack of a bait, and that were hard in this nibbling world where every man lays bait for another. In the city, merchants bait their tongues with a lie and an oath, and so make simple men swallow deceitful wares; 195 and fishing for commodity is grown so far that men are become fishes, for landlords put such sweet baits on rack rents that as good it were to be a perch in a pike's belly as a tenant in their farms. All our trade is grown to treachery, for now fish are caught with

---

185. at a table ... long] *Hent; not in Shent.*   186. evening] *Shent;* beginning *Hent.*
192. an] *Shent;* and *Hent.*

---

184. *walks*] See line 80n.
187–8. *a goodly fish pond*] Heaton notes that 'A pond called south pond adjoins Closewalks Wood' and that 'this is probably where this device was performed' (*Nichols*, iii, p. 558 n. 139).
188. *Angler*] Fisherman.
191. *Next rowing ... angling*] Though glossed by Heaton as 'Soon I will be rowing people upstream on the Thames ... angling farewell' (*Nichols*, p. 558 n. 140), and by Wilson (p. 159 n. 42), as 'going westward along the Thames (towards Westminster, the Queen's centre, from the City)', it seems more likely in view of what follows that the ironic exclamation signifies 'As against [*Next*] rowing a barge against the tide [*in a western barge*], angling might well be commended [*well fare angling*]', i.e. angling is the better of two supremely tiring and unrewarding occupations. The comment depends on the fact that the Thames flows from west to east. Compare Lyly's *Endymion*, 4.2.57–63, in which a similar formulation occurs.
193. *nibbling*] predatory.
195. *simple*] unsuspecting.
195. *swallow deceitful wares*] become consumers of fraudulent goods.
196. *fishing for commodity*] seeking means to make a profit.
197. *rack*] extortionate.
198. *perch*] common spiny-finned freshwater fish.
pike's belly] stomach of a fish noted for its predatory nature.
199–201. *for now ... unfortunate*] among the most significant of a series of echoes of Lyly's work (cf. 'fish caught with medicines and women gotten with witchcraft are never wholesome': *England*, p. 251) serving to suggest his authorship of the work (see pp. 25–6 above).

THE ENTERTAINMENT AT COWDRAY 39

medicines, which are as unwholesome as love procured by witchcraft unfortunate. We anglers make our lines of divers colours, according to the kinds of waters, so do men their loves, aiming at the complexion of the faces. Thus merchants, love and lordships suck venom out of virtue. I think I shall fish all day and catch a frog. The cause is neither in the line, the hook, nor the bait, but something there is over-beautiful, which stayeth the very minnow, of all fish the most eager, from biting. For this we anglers observe, that the shadow of a man turneth back the fish. What will, then, the sight of a goddess? 'Tis best angling in a lowering day, for here the sun so glisters that the fish see my hook through my bait. – But soft, here be the Netters. These be they that cannot content them with a dish of fish for their supper, but will draw a whole pond for the market.

This said, he espied a fisherman drawing his nets toward where Her Majesty was, and calling aloud to him –

'Ho, Sirrah', quoth the Angler, 'What shall I give thee for thy draught?'
'If there be never a whale in it, take it for a noble', quoth the Netter.
Angler. Be there any maids there?
Netter. Maids, fool? They be sea fish.
Angler. Why?

---

213. the] *Shent;* a *Hent.*

---

200. *medicines*] drugs, poisons.
unwholesome] prejudicial to health.
204. *suck ... virtue*] turn things that are potentially life-enhancing (e.g. food) into something destructive (as when tainted by poison).
204–5. *fish all ... frog*] proverbial for a fruitless endeavour (Tilley, F767).
206. *something there is over-beautiful*] i.e. the brilliance of the Queen's presence.
stayeth] stops, prevents.
209. *lowering*] overcast.
211. *soft*] quiet for a moment.
Netters] fishermen using a net to haul in a number of fish, rather than an angler using rod and line.
212–13. *draw a ... market*] trawl an entire pond to catch fish for sale.
217. *draught*] catch.
218. *never a whale*] no very large fish.
noble] former gold coin worth 6s 8d (a third of a pound).
220. *maids*] type of salt water fish (= skate or thornback ray).

Netter. Venus was born of the sea, and 'tis reason she should have maids to attend her.

Then turned he to the Queen, and after a small pause spake as followeth:

Madam, it is an old saying, 'There is no fishing to the sea, nor service to the king', but it holds when the sea is calm and the king virtuous. Your virtue maketh Envy blush, and stand amazed at your happiness. I come not to tell the art of fishing, nor the natures of fish, nor their daintiness, but with a poor fisherman's wish that all the hollow hearts to Your Majesty were in my net, and if there be more than it will hold, I would they were in the sea till I went thither a-fishing. There be some so muddy-minded that they cannot live in a clear river but a standing pool. As camels will not drink till they have troubled the water with their feet, so can they never staunch their thirst till they have disturbed the state with their treacheries. Soft! These are no fancies for fishermen. – Yes, true hearts are as good as full purses, the one the sinews of war, the other the arms. A dish of fish is an unworthy present for a prince to accept. There be some carps amongst them, no carpers of states.

---

229. maketh Envy ... stand] *Hent;* doth make Enuie blush, and Enuie stands *Shent.*

223. *Venus was ... sea*] Though ultimately derived from Ovid (*Venus orta mari: Heroides,* XV, 213), the immediate source of the phrase may be Lyly's *Sappho and Phao* (1.1.69–72), or the related play *Galatea* (5.1.50).
225. *he*] i.e. the Netter.
227–8. *There is ... the king*] proverbial saying (Tilley, F336), signifying that there is no type of fishing comparable with fishing in the sea and no form of service comparable with service to the king. The proverb formed the refrain of a song performed during the Queen's visit to Harefield in 1602, but had clearly been incorporated into a popular song at an earlier date (cf. Robert Greene, *James IV* (1590?), 'Now may I say, as many often sing, "No fishing to the sea, nor service to a king"' (1.2.39–40).
228. *holds*] holds good, i.e. is valid.
235–6. *camels ... feet*] proverbial saying (Tilley, C29), said by Giovanni Torriano (*Italian Proverbs,* 1666) to derive from the belief that camels could not bear to see their own deformity reflected in the water. The image is used by Lyly on a number of occasions in the context of social or political unrest (cf. *Mother Bombie,* 5.3.253–5; *Pap with an Hatchet,* 'To the Indifferent Reader', lines 14–16).
237. *staunch*] quench.
238. *These are ... fishermen*] It is not appropriate for men of my class to speculate about such matters.
240–1. *A dish ... accept*] The comment draws together the practice of offering gifts to the monarch in the course of her progress and the well-known story, related by Plutarch in 'The Sayings of Kings' and retailed by Erasmus (*Apophthegmata,* 'Antigonus', no. 15), turning on the appropriate value of gifts between ruler and subject. In this instance, the fisherman's catch is too modest to be a fit present for a monarch.
241. *carps ... carpers*] freshwater fish / those given to criticism or complaint.

If there be, I would they might be handled like carps, their tongues pulled out. Some perches there are, I am sure, and if any perch higher than in duty they ought, I would they might suddenly peak over the perch for me. Whatsoever there is, if it be good, it is all 245 yours, most virtuous Lady, that are best worthy of all.

Then was the net drawn. That ended, this song of the Fisherman:

> The fish that seeks for food in silver stream
>   Is, unawares, beguiled with the hook,
> And tender hearts, when least of love they dream,   250
>   Do swallow beauty's bait a lovely look.
> The fish that shuns to bite in net doth hit,
>   The heart that 'scapes the eye is caught by wit.
>
> The thing called love poor fishermen do feel,
>   Rich pearls are found in hard and homely shells,   255
> Our habits base, but hearts as true as steel,
>   Sad looks, deep sighs, flat faith are all our spells,
> And when to us our loves seem fair to be,
>   We court them thus, 'Love me, and I'll love thee'.
>
> And if they say our love is fondly made,   260
>   We never leave till on their hearts we light;
> Anglers have patience by their proper trade,
>   And are content to tarry till they bite.

244. peak] *This ed.*; picke *Hent, Shent*. 246. virtuous] *Hent*; excellent *Shent*. 246. all] *Hent*; the greatest good *Shent*. 247. Then was ... drawn.] *Hent*; not in *Shent*. 247–65. That ended ... at love] *Shent*; not in *Hent*.

---

242. *handled like*] treated in the same way as.
242–3. *their tongues pulled out*] Flesh-like in their consistency, carps' tongues were traditionally regarded as a delicacy and served independent of the fish.
243. *perches*] See line 198n.
244–5. *I would they ... for me*] 'For my part, I wish they would come to a quick end' (*peak over the perch* = hawking term, signifying to die: *OED*, v. I b, 'to topple or tumble off the perch').
247. *That ended*] That (i.e. the drawing of the net) being done.
250. *when least of love they dream*] when love is the last thing on their minds.
252. *in net doth hit*] swims into the net.
257. *flat faith*] plain, unqualified fidelity.
260. *they*] those we love. Also at line 263.
fondly made] foolish.
261. *leave*] desist.
on their ... light] we achieve their love.
262. *by their ... trade*] by virtue of their particular occupation.
263. *they*] (*a*) the fish (*b*) those whose love they seek to win.

> Of all the fish that in the waters move,
> We count them lumps that will not bite at love. 265

The Netter, having presented all the fish of the pond and laying it at her feet, departed. That evening she hunted.

THURSDAY

On Thursday she dined in the privy walks in the garden, and the lords and ladies, at a table of forty-eight yards long. In the evening, the 270 country people presented themselves to Her Majesty in a pleasant dance with tabor and pipe, and the Lord Montague and his lady among them, to the great pleasure of all the beholders and gentle applause of Her Majesty.

FRIDAY 275

On Friday she departed towards Chichester. Going through the arbour to take horse, stood six gentlemen, whom Her Majesty knighted, the Lord Admiral laying the sword on their shoulders. The names of the six knights then made were these, *viz*:

> Sir George Browne, my lord's second son. 280
> Sir Robert Dormer, his son-in-law.
> Sir Henry Goring.
> Sir Henry Glemham.
> Sir John Caryll.
> Sir Nicholas Parker. 285

266–91. *The Netter ... Valete*] Hent; *not in Shent which concludes* For the rest of the Entertainment, honorable feasting, and abundance of all things that might manifest a liberall and a loyall heart, because I was not there, I cannot set downe, thus much by report I heare, & by the words of those that deserue credite, that it was such as much contented her Maiestie, and made many others to wonder. And so her Maiestie well pleased with her welcome, & he throughly comforted with her Highnesse gracious acceptance, shee went from thence to Chichester. 280. *my lord's*] *This ed.*; my L. Hent; my Lordship's Heaton (Nichols, *iii*).

---

265. *lumps*] (*a*) dull creatures; (*b*) spiny, lead-blue freshwater fish.
269. *privy*] private, secluded.
272. *tabor*] small drum.
278. *Lord Admiral*] See line 50n.
281. *his son-in-law*] See line 38 and 38n.
282–5. *Sir Henry Goring ... Parker*] members of powerful interconnected Sussex families, all but *Goring* (a son of the holder of the lucrative office of Receiver General of the Court of Wards) with known or suspected Catholic affiliations. *Glemham*, eldest son of Thomas Glemham of Glemham Hall, was arrested after a visit to Rome in 1600 following a meeting with the Jesuit Robert Persons; *Caryll* was related to Montague through the Dormer family; For Sir Nicholas Parker see below.

So departed Her Majesty to the dining place, whither the Lord Montague and his sons, and the Sheriff of the Shire, attended with a goodly company of gentlemen, brought Her Highness.

The escutcheons on the oak remain and there shall hang till they can hang together, one piece by another. 290

Valete.

---

287. *Sheriff of the Shire*] The sovereign's representative for law, order, and the judiciary, and first in precedence in the county. The Sheriff's presence at the dinner heightens the emphasis placed throughout the visit on county loyalty and cohesion (cf. *attended with a goodly company of gentlemen*, lines 287–8). Sir Nicholas Parker was appointed to the office in 1592.

291. *Valete*] Farewell.

THE ENTERTAINMENT AT ELVETHAM

'The Great Pond in Elvetham'. Reproduced by kind permission of the Royal Collection Trust / © Her Majesty Queen Elizabeth II, 2017 (RCIN 1024755)

INTRODUCTION

The jewel in the crown of the events mounted for the royal progress in the course of the 1590s was undoubtedly the entertainment devised for the Queen's visit to Edward Seymour, 1st Earl of Hertford, at Elvetham in north-east Hampshire, in late September 1591. Like Viscount Montague, her host at Cowdray the previous month (see p. 18ff.), Seymour occupied a somewhat uneasy position in relation to the monarch in that his father had been executed for treason in 1552, while he himself had entered into a secret marriage in 1560 with Katherine Grey, a younger sister of Lady Jane Grey and great-granddaughter of Henry VII, and thus a pretender to the throne.[1] To marry a member of the royal family without the monarch's consent constituted a penal offence, and when the news of their marriage leaked out the couple were confined to the Tower, where Katherine remained until her death. Though Hertford reinstated himself in court circles to some degree following his release in 1563, his return to public life did not signal a full rapprochement with the Crown,[2] and doubts regarding his loyalty were rekindled when his eldest son, himself a potential claimant to the throne,[3] also married without the monarch's consent. Given Elizabeth's growing sensitivity to the implications of her advancing age and gathering anxiety in the 1590s at her failure to acknowledge an heir to the throne, generating fears of a disputed succession, it was a matter of prime importance for Hertford to assure the monarch of his good faith and the absolute nature of his devotion to her service.

A number of factors appeared to militate against the provision of an entertainment sufficiently lavish to banish any suspicion on the part of the sovereign of latent disloyalty to the Crown. As the anonymous compiler of a contemporary account of the event noted,[4] the Earl was largely reliant on 'the ordinary guess' (i.e. the Lord Chamberlain's itinerary), together with information gleaned by 'his honourable good friends in the court', for advance notice of when the visit was scheduled to take place (see lines 12–13), and the former had not been finalized until mid-July, allowing him only two months in which to prepare.[5] To compound his problems, Elvetham, with its relatively small park, of but 'two miles in compass or thereabouts', and low income from rents, was not one of his 'chief mansion houses', and thus hardly suited to exhibiting the 'unfeigned love and loyal duty to her most gracious Highness' (lines 8–11) that the occasion plainly required. The seemingly peripheral information regarding the extensive work undertaken prior to the monarch's arrival, recorded in the first published account of the visit, is thus intrinsic to an understanding of the entertainment as a whole, affording an insight into the titanic organizational endeavour that the success of the stay represented.

An army of workmen numbering 'two hundred or thereabouts' (line 15) and including a variety of skilled craftsmen was assembled to address the problem of accommodating not only the monarch herself and the members of her court but the innumerable attendants involved in the royal progress. Rooms for a wide variety of purposes were constructed a short distance from the sovereign's apartments in the main house, including a richly ornamented state room for the reception of the nobility, a hall for indoor entertainments, a dining hall for the Earl's steward, rooms for upper and lower servants, a suite of utility rooms designed to cater for large numbers of diners, and provision for Her Majesty's guards. While the building work was in progress, detailed planning for a series of highly elaborate entertainments clearly took place, in that a further group of workmen was assembled for the construction of a crescent-shaped lake, positioned between the mansion house and the new buildings, and large enough to accommodate three precisely positioned islands, with appropriate vegetation, representing a fort, a ship, and a snail (see illustration on p. 46).[6] The detailed planning of the feature is indicative that the principal entertainment to be performed there had been fully thought out before the work was begun, and the furnishing of the three islands with cannon and a variety of fireworks confirms that the entertainments on the first and third days of the visit had been devised at the same time.

Arrangements for the monarch's formal reception must also have been undertaken while the building work was under way. A long welcoming speech in Latin, probably by Thomas Watson,[7] was commissioned for the occasion, and an emblematic costume and appropriate accoutrements prepared for the speaker who was required to master and deliver the lines. A welcoming show was devised to accompany the oration, in the form of six elaborately costumed virgins, representing the Graces and the Hours, 'with flowery garlands on their heads, and baskets full of sweet herbs and flowers upon their arms' (lines 268–70) removing symbolic obstacles from the monarch's path and singing a further piece, probably by Watson, as they preceded her to the house. Similar preparations for the staging of the much more extensive show to be performed on and around the lake on the second day of the visit must also have been put in hand as soon as the date of the sovereign's arrival was known, including the devising of the action, the composition of speeches, the casting of parts (presumably from members of the Earl's own acting troupe), the construction of a variety of vessels, the provision of a large number of elaborate costumes, and the rehearsal of the complex manoeuvres to be executed on the water once the construction of the lake and its islands was sufficiently advanced.

Forward planning was not confined, moreover, to the provision of suitable accommodation, the reshaping of the landscape, and the commissioning of a variety of shows. As noted above, munitions were installed on the Snail Mount and the Ship Isle, both to salute the monarch's arrival and to celebrate her presence on the third day of her visit by means of a 'peal of an hundred chambers' (line 610) from one island echoed by a similar volley from another – an effect enhanced by the firing of cannon. A spectacular firework show involving a variety of effects, including balls of fire seemingly burning on the water, and rockets running from one island to another, was devised to follow the firing of the munitions, and both the fireworks themselves and the mechanism for their firing must have been installed on the islands while rehearsals for the pageant were under way. A group of Somerset men was assembled to play at board-and-cord under the Queen's window, while the gifts to be presented to the monarch at intervals throughout the visit,[8] including a 'fair and rich gift' (line 327) from the Countess of Hertford and two jewels presented in the course of the pageant on the lake, must also have been commissioned at an early stage in the preparations to allow adequate time for their creation.

The diversions planned for Her Majesty's entertainment were not confined, moreover, to the customary 'shows'. A banquet consisting of more than a thousand dishes, carried in procession by 'two hundred of my Lord of Hertford's gentlemen' (lines 621–2), accompanied by a hundred torch-bearers, was scheduled as a finale to the penultimate day of the stay, requiring not only the assembling and careful coaching of adequate staff but the preparation of innumerable items of sugar-work, ranging from the coat of arms of the monarch to representations of every branch of the animal kingdom, from 'Lions, unicorns, bears, horses, camels, bulls, rams, dogs, tigers, elephants, antelopes, dromedaries, apes, and all other beasts' 'to 'Snakes, adders, vipers, frogs, toads, and all kind of worms' (lines 632–8), together with a variety of crustaceans, and 'comfits, of all sorts' (lines 648–9). Foodstuffs sufficient to testify to 'the plentiful abundance' (line 314) of the host's provisions throughout the visit must also have been requisitioned while the culinary preparations were in hand, and marshalled in the newly constructed storage facilities once the building work was complete.

While the sugar-rich banquet was clearly designed to cater to the Queen's sweetness of tooth, attention was also paid to her more sophisticated tastes. Throughout her visit the house and grounds were suffused with music, plainly designed not merely to delight a monarch fully capable of appreciating the virtuosity of the performers but to exhibit the refinement of her host. A consort of six highly accomplished musicians was assembled in readiness for her arrival, in order to perform whenever she desired, and a variety of pieces, both novel and familiar, were commissioned to accompany the visual effects. The singing of a madrigal by the Graces and the Hours on the Queen's entrance to the park, for example, implied that Hertford was attuned to contemporary continental musical developments, in that very few madrigals by English composers had been published when the visit took place,[9] while a long-familiar pavan by Thomas Morley, performed on the evening of the same day, so 'highly pleased' (line 320) the Queen by its execution that she gave it a new name – suggesting the piece had been well rehearsed. Lunch on the second day of the stay was accompanied by a 'variety of consorted music' (line 340), while a song remarkable, in Katherine Butler's words, for the 'logistical complexity'[10] of its performance formed a notable feature of the water pageant that took place in the afternoon.[11]

The third and fourth days of the visit also featured sung pieces that appear to have afforded the Queen particular pleasure. Another madrigal, 'In the Merry Month of May', performed by 'three excellent musicians' (lines 563–4) under her gallery window, earned the singers not only 'cheerful acceptance and commendation' (lines 568–9) but the honour of a request for it to be performed for a second time. Similarly, a quasi-balletic show enacted in the same location on the final day of her stay, involving three cornets (see line 364n. below) playing 'fantastic dances' (line 653), the Fairy Queen 'dancing with her maids about her' (line 654), and a piece in 'six parts, with the music of an exquisite consort' (lines 676–7) performed in the course of yet another elaborate dance, so delighted the monarch that she asked 'to hear it sung and to be danced three times over, and called for divers lords and ladies to behold it' (lines 692–3). Even the sovereign's departure was marked by a striking, carefully orchestrated musical effect. Two distinguished singers, accompanied by a consort of musicians concealed in a bower at the entrance to the park, urged the monarch to 'Come Again' (line 740), with the wistful air seeming to arise from the landscape itself, rather than being the product of human design.[12]

Though at first sight the number and variety of diversions mounted in the course of the visit might suggest that *Elvetham* falls into a series of discrete units rather than being conceived as an organic whole, in fact one of the most impressive aspects of the piece is the unity of conception underlying its seemingly diverse sequence of rapidly assembled events. The visit is structured from the outset in quasi-dramatic terms, with the monarch cast as a deity whose beneficence transforms both the human and physical worlds. The concept of performance is introduced in the opening lines of the first published account of the event, which note that, prior to riding with his followers to escort the monarch to the house, Hertford schooled them in the demeanour they were to assume during Her Majesty's stay, adding that the majority of them had 'chains of gold about their necks, and in their hats Yellow and Black feathers',[13] suggesting the assumption of costumes and roles. The implication that in arriving at Elvetham the monarch was stepping on to a stage is sustained by a reference to the 'near ten thousand people' (line 109) gathered to witness her arrival at the park, and by the welcoming address of the costumed Poet equating her with a series of supernatural beings and authority figures whose influence reverses the post-lapsarian condition. Her translation into a divinity, and Elvetham into an Arcadian world, is sustained in her advance towards the house, in that the Hours and Graces who form her escort are not only 'Virtue's maids' and the 'guardians of heaven's gate' (lines 251-2) but the traditional companions of Venus, implying that she enters the house as the goddess of love. The ensuing diversions similarly align her with further classical deities and powerful beings from folklore and myth. On the second day of the visit, for example, marine spirits salute her as Cynthia, 'the wide Ocean's Empress' (line 395), and a pastoral figure (Sylvanus) expresses his 'holy fear' (line 489) in her presence. The sugar-work banquet on the evening of the third day of her visit denotes her sovereignty over the natural world, while she is saluted by the Fairy Queen on the morning of her departure, as 'Bright-shining Phoebe' (line 669), and honoured by her with song and dance. The Queen is not merely a passive spectator, moreover, of the shows in which her divinity is affirmed. She is positioned as an active participant in the fictions, implicitly endorsing their implications by her involvement, and by the actions she is called on to perform. In approaching the house in the conduct of the Graces and the Hours, for example, she enacts the role of the goddess of love, while in naming Neaera's ship in the course of the pageant on the lake, and accepting the scutcheon supposedly devised by Apollo, she becomes an actor in, rather than a spectator of, the unfolding drama, with the entire park transformed into a species of stage. Similarly, as the recipient of the Fairy Queen's tribute of a garland 'in form of an imperial crown' (line 655) she implicitly confirms her sovereignty over 'places under ground' (line 659), and the reality of a metaphysical universe over which her supremacy extends. The closing scene of the entertainment, in which the fictional beings of the preceding shows come together to mourn her departure from the house, reinforces the sense of Elvetham as a location divorced from the everyday world, with the monarch located among, and interacting with an entire assembly of mythical beings, while the closing song laments the fallen condition signalled by the conclusion of her stay.

The repeated endorsements of the quasi-divine status of the sovereign, together with the elaborate gifts presented in the course of the visit, and the pointed attention to her personal tastes were plainly designed, not simply to gratify and delight the monarch, but as a means of ingratiation on the part of her host, exhibiting the totality of his commitment to the Elizabethan regime, and his readiness to expend his every resource in the Queen's service. The opening address, for example, emphasizes that his happiness and peace of mind are entirely dependent upon his assurance of her good will; the ensuing reception of her as Venus defines him as one whose home is a place of love; the pageant on the lake aligns him with forces dedicated to her security and the success of her reign; while even the pastoral ditty sung beneath her gallery window on the third day of the visit turns on a relationship founded on enduring affection and trust. While some progress receptions require a degree of mental agility on the part of the audience in order to decode the fictions that they present, here the Poet's overt declaration at the outset that 'Under my person Seymour hides himself' (line 222) ensures that his desire to position himself as a devoted servant of the monarch is plain from the outset to all, from the sovereign to whom the oration was originally addressed, through her attendants, to those perusing the text published immediately after the entertainment took place.

Unfortunately, while the conceptual world evoked by the Elvetham entertainment was plainly designed to situate the visit (and thus the relationship between monarch and subject) on an idyllic, ethereal plane, the actuality proved analogous, for both spectators and performers, to that of many twenty-first-century British productions of Shakespeare in the park. As H. Neville Davies reminds us, though the stay took place between 20 and 23 September, 'had our Gregorian calendar then been in operation the visit would have crossed the threshold into what is now regarded as October',[14] and the weather amply conformed to current views regarding what might be expected of the climate at that date. The morning of the second day of the visit 'was so wet and stormy that nothing of pleasure could be presented to Her Majesty' and had it not 'held up a little before dinner time, and all the day after ... fair sports would have been buried in foul weather' (lines 329–32). As it was, conditions for the audience at the pageant on the lake (the entertainment devised for the late afternoon) must have been uncomfortable to say the least, while the unfortunate performers, required to swim or wade through the lake and then stand for a lengthy period in the breast-high water, were plainly obliged to perform their celebratory roles in a decidedly miserable physical state. Similarly, the Poet's assertion that summer would give way to autumn with the monarch's departure from the estate was borne out by the 'most extreme rain' (lines 697–8 SN) in which the mythical beings were obliged to make their farewells, lending a painfully apposite force to his evocation of their 'showers of tears' and 'wet lament' (lines 713 and 714).

The philosophy underpinning the institution of the royal progress is summed up in Hertford's address to his servants prior to Her Majesty's arrival at the house. Drawing them into 'the chief thicket of the park ... he put them in mind what quietness, and what diligence or other duty they were to use at that present, that their service might first work Her Majesty's content and thereby his honour, and lastly their own credit, with the increase of his love and favour toward them' (lines 94–8). The circulation of social benefit defined by the exhortation provided the motivating force behind the endeavours of all those engaged in the peregrinations of the monarch, justifying both the financial and physical costs, and the rich rewards bestowed on the performers by the monarch at Elvetham must undoubtedly have fulfilled their expectations in that respect. It must have been of some comfort to Hertford himself, moreover, that the physical endurance required of his actors by the adverse conditions was met by the resilience (and magnanimity) of their ageing Queen. The text records that, for all the dampness and fading light, the pastime on the lake was to her 'so great liking ... that her gracious approbation thereof was to the actors more than a double reward' (lines 557–9), while the rain-sodden farewells were also received with a generous show of appreciation. Side-notes in the second edition of the text affirm that for all the 'extreme rain ... it pleased Her Majesty with great patience to behold and hear the whole action' (lines 697–702 SN) and that 'notwithstanding the great rain [she] stayed her coach and pulled off her mask' to listen to the closing song at the park gate, 'giving great thanks' to the musicians (lines 746–50 SN). The unfeigned nature of the monarch's enjoyment is indicated, moreover, by her response to the masque of the Fairy Queen performed on the morning of the same day. Though conditions could hardly have been conducive to a polished performance, she was so delighted by the music and spectacle that she asked, as previously noted, for it to be performed three times, and richly rewarded those involved at the close.

For all the inclement weather, the vast effort and expense involved in mounting the entertainment may also have seemed worthwhile to Hertford himself, fulfilling his own hopes of fortifying his position. According to the author of the account of the entertainment published the following month, the Queen was 'so highly pleased' by her reception that she publicly informed him 'that the beginning, process, and end of this his entertainment was so honourable that she would not forget the same' (lines 752-5). His subsequent career does not suggest, however, that his hopes were fulfilled.[15]

A NOTE ON THE TEXT

However successful the event in terms of securing the monarch's approval, the stormy weather must necessarily have blunted audience awareness of the many nuances of an intricate entertainment, cohering around a single theme and extending over a number of days, and it may well have been the desire to permit a more leisurely appreciation of the complexities of the piece by those to whom it was initially directed, as well as to promote Hertford's standing in the eyes of a wider audience, that motivated the publication of what was plainly an authorized account of the work.[16] *The Honorable Entertainement gieuen to the Queenes Maiestie in Progresse, at Eluetham in Hampshire, by the right Honorable the Earle of Hertford* (Q1) was entered in the Stationers' Register within days of the conclusion of the visit, and appeared on the bookstalls in the course of the following weeks.[17] The text was accompanied by a large fold-out sheet illustrating the water pageant, with the salient features keyed to the author's account of the construction of the lake (see Proem, lines 63-76), and further information (e.g. the Earl's exhortation to his followers prior to the monarch's arrival: lines 89-98) was supplied in a 'Newlie corrected, and amended' edition (Q2) of the event published before the end of the year.

Though some contemporary readers were consequently furnished with an unusually detailed insight into the pastimes of the aristocratic elite, and others with an enduring record of an essentially evanescent event, subsequent generations, paradoxically, have been progressively less well served in the course of the editorial history of the text. By the close of the eighteenth century, no copy of the more authoritative of the two quartos (Q2) was known to exist, and the first edition of the work subsequent to its initial publication, edited by Richard Gough for the *Gentleman's Magazine* in 1779, was consequently based on Q1. More damaging in terms of promoting an understanding of the event, the fold-out map accompanying the text of the authorized edition was replaced by a reproduction, in which a host of misleading and anachronistic features were introduced. The drawing was subsequently included by John Nichols in his *Progresses of Queen Elizabeth I* (1788), but publication of the volume was delayed by his discovery of a copy of Q2, and a further redrawn copy of the woodcut was commissioned, derived (with significant alterations) from the more authoritative of the two sixteenth-century editions. The book was eventually issued with both eighteenth-century versions of the woodcut, and an addendum noting what Nichols regarded as the most significant discrepancies between the texts of Q1 and Q2. It was the second of these two redrawn versions of the illustration, rather than a reproduction of the woodcut itself, which Nichols subsequently incorporated into his monumental *The Progresses and Public Processions of Queen Elizabeth I* (1823) from which the majority of subsequent editions of *Elvetham* derive, and, since Q2 was again lost to view in the early nineteenth century an erroneous pictorial record of the event has consequently been transmitted from text to text for nearly two hundred years.

Equally damaging in terms of modern understanding of the work was Nichols's attempt to incorporate the additional material from Q2, noted at the close of his 1788 edition, into the main body of his 1823 text. As Davies points out, 'the textual adjustments [were] accomplished without any fresh recourse to either *Q1* or *Q2* themselves',[18] leading R. Warwick Bond, the next significant editor of the work, to be confused by the ensuing errors into the belief that there were three rather than two sixteenth-century editions,[19] a belief that has continued to haunt the work, for all its implicit repudiation by W.W. Greg,[20] into the twenty-first century.[21] Since all later editions, prior to the publication of the revised edition of Nichols's work in 2014, looked back either to the version published by Nichols himself in 1823, or to one or other of the surviving copies of Q1, and were frequently accompanied by one of the two eighteenth-century illustrations, no twentieth-century edition of the work can be said to offer the reader an authoritative account of the events of late September 1591. It was the chance discovery by H. Neville Davies of a reproduction of the Q2 site map in Edmund H. Fellowes, *The English Madrigal* (1925) – alerting him to the fact that a copy of the second quarto was still in existence in the early twentieth century – and the ensuing detective work that led him to the location of a hitherto unknown copy in the Royal Library at Windsor,[22] that finally enabled the publication of an accurate edition of the work. It is on this edition by Davies, published, appropriately, in the new five-volume *Nichols*, that the text in this collection is primarily based, though both the first and second quartos have been independently consulted.

Though *Elvetham* is among the more frequently published Elizabethan entertainments, and has previously appeared in a number of modern-spelling editions, its inclusion in the present volume is warranted by the checkered history of the text. No previous modern-spelling edition looks back directly to Q2 (the fullest account of the event) or reproduces its authoritative site map, and none could rely on the scholarly investigation mounted by Davies into the circumstances governing the production of the work. At the same time, the provision of extensive notes, in contrast to the practice of previous editions, is designed to facilitate engagement with an unfamiliar art form, rather than merely to explicate obsolete terms, while the employment of an uncomplicated system of reference (through line numbering) is designed to enable ease of discussion. It is hoped, in short, that the inclusion of the text in this volume will help to further understanding of a remarkably inventive work, rather than contributing to the progressive obfuscation of one of the most ambitious of sixteenth-century attempts to secure a monarch's goodwill.

NOTES

1 Under the will of Henry VIII the offspring of his younger sister, Mary, took precedence over those of his elder sister, Margaret. As the eldest surviving descendant of Mary, Lady Jane Grey had thus a strong claim to the throne given the dubious legitimacy of both Mary I and Elizabeth herself. Seymour's offence was compounded by the fact that he himself was a cousin of Edward VI, and consequently a member of the wider royal house.
2 A number of constraints were placed on him and he was subject to a heavy fine.
3 Though both of Seymour's sons by Katherine had been declared illegitimate during their mother's lifetime, they remained a potential threat to both Elizabeth herself and the security of the Stuart succession.
4 *The Honorable Entertainement gieuen to the Queenes Maiestie in Progresse, at Eluetham in Hampshire, by the right Honorable the Earle of Hertford* (1591).
5 See Davies, p. 231.
6 For an illuminating discussion of the symmetrical construction of the lake and its aesthetic implications, see Davies, pp. 233ff.
7 A distinguished lyric poet, celebrated for both his work in Latin and his innovatory poetic forms, Watson was declared by Frances Meres in his *Palladis Tamia* (1598) to be the equal of Petrarch, Theocritus, and Virgil.
8 The commissioning of appropriate gifts for the monarch was a matter of considerable concern for prospective hosts and a failure to gratify all members of the royal household was regarded with particular disfavour. Sir William Clarke of Burnham, for example, was widely reported to 'haue so behaued himself that he pleased no body, but gaue occasion to haue his miserie [i.e. miserliness] and vanitie spread far and wide' (quoted from *Nichols*, iv, p. 202).
9 See Butler, p. 155.
10 Butler, p. 155.
11 The text notes that the piece was sung 'dialogue-wise' (line 439) to the lute by 'three voices in the pinnace ... with excellent divisions, and the end of every verse was replied by lutes and voices in the other boat somewhat afar off, as if they had been echoes' (lines 434–7) – an effect that would have required considerable rehearsal once both the lake and vessels were available for use.
12 Appropriately, the entertainment was commemorated, some four hundred years after the Queen's visit, by a performance by a group of six musicians (the Sneyd Consort), dressed in Elizabethan costumes, playing a selection of sixteenth-century music on instruments that would have been familiar to a contemporary spectator

(viols, crumhorns, and recorders). The musical items were interspersed with readings from sixteenth-century works and may have included sung or spoken material from the copy of Q1 preserved in the library at Lambeth Palace. (I am indebted to Professor Stephen Banfield, who participated in the event, for supplying me with this information.)
13 *The Honorable Entertainement gieuen to the Queenes Maiestie in Progresse, at Eluetham* (1591), A4r. The second edition of the work, published in the same year, differs with regard to the number of followers in the escort and omits all mention of the yellow and black feathers.
14 Davies, p. 211.
15 He was imprisoned again in 1595 following an attempt to secure the legitimacy of his sons.
16 The author repeatedly refers to Hertford as 'my lord' and writes from the standpoint of an informed observer, suggesting that he held a position in the Earl's entourage.
17 Three copies of Q1 (all with minor textual variants) are known to survive: in Lambeth Place Library (LPL ZZ.1593.28.97), Cambridge University Library (CUL Bb*.11.50(E)), and the British Library (BL C33.e.7.(9)).
18 *Nichols*, iii, p. 565.
19 See Bond, i, p. 431n.
20 See *A Bibliography of the English Printed Drama to the Restoration* (London, 1939, reprinted 1970), i, item 98.
21 See, for example, Donald Stump and Susan M. Felch, eds, *Elizabeth I and Her Age*, A Norton Critical Edition (New York and London, 2009), p. 417n.
22 See Davies, *passim*.

THE ENTERTAINMENT AT ELVETHAM

THE PROEM

Before I declare the just time or manner of Her Majesty's arrival and entertainment at Elvetham, it is needful, for the reader's better understanding of every part and process in my discourse, that I set down as well the conveniency of the place as also the suffising by art and labour of what the place in itself could not afford on the sudden for receipt of so great a Majesty and so honourable a train.

Elvetham house being situate in a park but of two miles in compass or thereabouts, and of no great receipt, as being none of the Earl's chief mansion houses, yet for the desire he had to show his unfeigned love and loyal duty to her most gracious Highness purposing to visit him in this her late progress (whereof he had to understand by the ordinary guess, as also by his honourable good friends in the court near to Her Majesty), his Honour with all expedition set artificers a-work, to the number of two hundred or thereabouts, many days before Her

---

13. the court] *Q2*; court *Q1*.   15. two hundred or thereabouts] *Q2*; three hundred *Q1*.

---

1. *PROEM*] Preface.
2. *just*] precise.
3. *Elvetham*] a minor estate in the north-east of Hampshire, held by Edward Seymour, 1st Earl of Hertford, but not his principal seat (hence *none of the Earl's chief mansion houses*: lines 9–10). For the Earl of Hertford, see p. 47.
5. *conveniency*] suitability, fitness.
suffising] supplementing, making good.
6. *on the sudden*] in a brief time. Prospective hosts were frequently afforded little notice of the arrival of the monarch.
receipt of] receiving.
7. *so ... train*] such noble attendants.
8. *situate*] located.
compass] circumference.
9. *of no great receipt*] having no substantial income from rents.
12. *late*] recent.
whereof he had to understand] of which he was informed.
12–13. *ordinary guess*] Lord Chamberlain's itinerary listing the places the Queen intended to visit in the course of her progress. See Davies, *Nichols*, iii, p. 570n.
14–16. *his Honour ... offices*] A much more extensive account of the 'Roomes and Lodginges' provided for the monarch and her entourage for her visit to Theobalds in 1583 suggests that the preparations detailed in lines 22–44 were not unusual (see *Nichols*, iii, pp. 187–92).

Majesty's arrival, to enlarge his house with new rooms and offices; whereof I omit to speak how many were destined to the offices of the Queen's household, and will only make mention of other such buildings as were raised on the sudden fourteen score off from the house, on a hillside within the said park, for entertainment of nobles, gentlemen, and others whatsoever.

First there was made a Room of Estate for the nobles, and at the end thereof a withdrawing place for Her Majesty. The outsides of the walls were all covered with boughs and clusters of ripe hazel nuts; the inside with arras; the roof of the place with works of ivy leaves; the floor with sweet herbs and green rushes.

Near adjoining unto this were many other offices newly converted, as namely spicery, lardery, chandlery, wine cellar, ewery, and pantry; all which were tiled. Not far off was erected a large hall, for entertainment of knights, ladies, gentlemen and gentlewomen of chief account. There was also a several place for Her Majesty's footmen and their friends. Then was there a long bower for Her Majesty's guard; another for other servants of Her Majesty's house; another to entertain all comers, suitors, and such like; another for the Earl's steward to keep his table in; another for his gentlemen that waited. Most of these foresaid rooms were

---

25. inside] *Q2*; insides *Q1*. 27. other offices newly converted] *Q2*; offices new builded *Q1*. 30. gentlemen and gentlewomen] *Nichols (subst.)*; and Gentlemen *Q1*; and Gentlewomen *Q2*. 33. servants] *Q2*; Officers *Q1*. 33-4. another ... such like] *Q1*; *not in Q2*. 34. the Earl's] *Q2*; my Lords *Q1* (*also at line 45 below*).

---

16. *offices*] places dedicated to household concerns.
19. *fourteen score off*] two hundred and eighty paces away.
22. *Room of Estate*] large presence chamber for gatherings of the social elite.
23-4. *The outsides ... hazel nuts*] possibly decorative artworks, though an illusion of rusticity through the use of natural materials may have been contrived.
25. *arras*] richly coloured tapestries.
roof] ceiling. The decorative features were probably painted, rather than plasterwork, given the speed of construction.
26. *sweet ... rushes*] used as a sweet-smelling floor covering. The strewing of green rushes symbolized the reception of an honoured guest.
27. *converted*] adapted. Q1 states, by contrast, that these structures were *new builded* rather than *converted* (see collation note).
28. *lardery, chandlery ... ewery, and pantry*] store-rooms for meat, candles ... dining-table hand-washing equipment, and bread.
30. *chief account*] most importance.
31. *several*] separate.
33. *suitors*] those seeking to promote their affairs or present petitions.
34. *Earl's steward*] officer responsible for the smooth running of the Earl's household.
35. *waited*] served.

furnished with tables, and the tables carried three and twenty yards in length.

Moreover, on the same hill there was raised a great common buttery; a pitcher house; a large pastery, with five ovens new built, some of them fourteen foot deep; a great kitchen with four ranges, and a boiling place for small boiled meats; another kitchen with a very long range, for the waste, to serve all comers; a boiling house for the great boiler; a room for the scullery; another room for the cooks' lodgings. Some of these were covered with canvas, and other some with boards.

Between the Earl's house and the foresaid hill where these rooms were raised there had been made in the bottom, by handy labour, a goodly pond, cut to the perfect figure of a half moon. In this pond were three notable grounds, wherehence to present Her Majesty with sports and pastimes. The first was a Ship Isle, of one hundred foot in length and forty foot broad, bearing three trees, orderly set, for three masts. The second was a Fort, twenty foot square every way, and every flanker arboured with willows. The third and last was a Snail Mount, rising to four circles of green privy hedges, the whole in height twenty foot, and fourscore foot broad at the bottom. These three places were equally distant from the sides of the pond, and every one by a just measured proportion distant from other, and from the ends of the pond. In the said water were divers boats prepared for music; but especially there

---

51–2. every flanker arboured] Q2; ouergrown Q1. 54. fourscore] Q2; fortie Q1. 56. other ... the pond] Q2; other. Q1.

---

36. *carried*] extended.
38–9. *buttery ... pitcher*] store-room for foodstuffs in barrels (butts) ... large, lipped vessel used for the distribution of liquid refreshments.
39. *pastery*] place for the preparation of pastry.
42. *waste*] foodstuffs surplus to the entertainment of the principal guests.
43. *scullery*] place for the washing and storing of dishes and utensils.
46. *bottom*] low ground.
  handy] manual.
47. *pond*[1]] lake. (The dimensions that follow indicate that the feature was much larger than the term 'pond' suggests today.)
  perfect figure ... moon] For the significance of the crescent form of the lake, and the shape and disposition of the three islands (lines 49–56) see lines 38on., 381n., 391n., and 395n..
48. *grounds*] locations, sites.
50. *orderly set*] precisely arranged.
51. *flanker*] fortification placed to command the flanks of an enemy.
52. *arboured with*] shrouded by.
53. *four circles ... hedges*] i.e. designed to represent the shell of a snail (*privy* = privet).
55–6. *just measured ... other*] precisely measured equal distance from the others.
57. *divers*] a number of (also at line 61).

was a pinnace, full furnished with masts, yards, sails, anchors, cables, and all other ordinary tackling, and with iron pieces, and lastly with flags, streamers, and pendants, to the number of twelve, all painted with divers colours and sundry devices. To what use these particulars served it shall evidently appear by that which followeth.

> *A description of the great pond in Elvetham, and of the properties which it contained, at such time as Her Majesty was there presented with fair shows and pastimes.*

A. Her Majesty's presence seat, and train.
B. Nereus and his followers.
C. The pinnace of Neaera, and her music.
D. The Ship Isle.
E. A boat with music, attending on the pinnace of Neaera.
F. The Fort Mount.
G. The Snail Mount.
H. The Room of Estate.
I. Her Majesty's court.
K. Her Majesty's wardrobe.
L. The place whence Sylvanus and his companions issued.

And therefore I am to request the gentle reader that when any of these places are briefly specified in the sequel of this discourse, it will please him to have reference to this fore description; that in avoiding reiterations, I may not seem to them obscure whom I study to please with my

---

63–4.] Q2; *A Description ... containeth.* / Q1.   66–76.] *missing from surviving copies of Q1.*   79–80. reiterations] Q2; tantilogies, or reiterations Q1.

---

58. *pinnace*] light (usually eight-oared) vessel, attendant on a man-of-war.
yards] spars (for hanging sails).
59. *pieces*] cannon.
60. *pendants*] pennants.
61. *sundry*] a variety of.
66. A] The alphabetic listing of the locations functions as a key to the fold-out map accompanying the printed text (see p. 46). I and J being largely interchangeable at this date, the latter does not appear in the list.
presence seat] chair of state.
67. *Nereus*] wise marine deity, credited with the power of prophecy, and father of the fifty Nereides. He was frequently represented bearing a trident.
68. *Neaera*] a sea nymph (here the object of Sylvanus's affections).
75. *Her Majesty's wardrobe*] the office responsible for the care of the Queen's apparel.
76. *Sylvanus*] a god of the fields and woods (as his name implies), usually represented as a cheerful old man.

plainness. For Proem this may suffice. Now to the matter itself, that it may be *ultimum in executione* (to use the old phrase) *quod primum fuit in intentione*, as is usual to good carpenters who, intending to build a house, yet first lay their foundation, and square many a post, and fasten many a rafter, before the house be set up. What they first purposed, is last done. And thus much for excuse of a long foundation to a short building.

THE FIRST DAY'S ENTERTAINMENT

On the twentieth day of September, being Monday, the Earl of Hertford, joyfully expecting Her Majesty's coming to Elvetham to supper as Her Highness had promised, the same morning, about nine of the clock, when every other needful place or point of service was established and set in order for so great an entertainment, called for, and drew his servants into the chief thicket of the park, where in few words he put them in mind what quietness, and what diligence or other duty they were to use at that present, that their service might first work Her Majesty's content and thereby his honour, and lastly their own credit, with the increase of his love and favour toward them. This done, after dinner, with his train well mounted, to the number of two hundred and upwards, and most of them wearing chains of gold about their necks, he rode towards Odiham, and, leaving his train and company orderly

---

81. this] *Q2*; these *Q1*. 89. twentieth] *Q1* (twentith); twentie *Q2*. the Earl] *Q2*; my Lord *Q1* (*also at lines 105, 317, 341, and 598 below*). 91–104. the same morning ... Odiham house] *Q2*; after dinner, when euery other needful place or point of seruice was established and set in order, for so great an entertainment, about three of the clocke his Honor seing all his Retinew well mounted and ready to attend his pleasure, hee drew them secretly into a chief thicket of the Parke, where in few words, but well couched to the purpose, hee put them in mind, what quietnes, and what diligence, or other duetie they were to vse at that present: that their seruice might first work her Maiesties content, & thereby his Honor, and lastlie their own credite, with increse of his loue and fauour towards them. This done, my Lord with his traine (amounting to the number of 3. hundred, and most of them wearing chains of gold about their necks, and in their hats Yellow and Black feathers) met with her Maiestie two miles off, then comming to Eluetham from her owne house of Odiham four miles from thence *Q1*.

82–3. ultimum in executione ... quod primum fuit in intentione] '[be] at last in execution what it was initially in intention'. The axiom was ultimately derived from Thomas Aquinas (hence *to use the old phrase*).
88–104.] See collation note for the discrepancies between this account and that given in the first quarto.
90. *supper*] evening meal taken between 5 and 8 pm.
95. *quietness*] discreet orderliness.
95–6. *they were to use*] with which they were to conduct themselves.
96. *present*] time.
99. *dinner*] midday meal.
101. *Odiham*] manor house south of Elvetham, where the Queen had been a guest of Edward More. See Davies (*Nichols*, iii, p. 563n.).

placed to attend Her Majesty's coming out of Odiham park, three miles distant from Elvetham, himself waited on Her Majesty from Odiham house.

As the Earl in this first action showed himself dutiful, so Her Majesty was to him and his most gracious. As also in the sequel, between five and six of the clock, when Her Highness, being most honourably attended, entered into Elvetham park, where (to Her Majesty's great liking) were, by estimate, near ten thousand people from sundry places; and was more than half-way between the park gate and the house a Poet saluted her with a Latin oration in heroical verse. I mean *veridicus vates*, a soothsaying poet, nothing inferior for truth and little for delivery of his mind to an ordinary orator. This Poet was clad in green to signify the joy of his thoughts at her entrance; a laurel garland on his head, to express that Apollo was patron of his studies; an olive branch in his hand, to declare what continual peace and plenty he did both wish and abode Her Majesty; and lastly booted to betoken that he was *vates cothurnatus*, and not a loose or low creeping prophet, as poets are interpreted by some idle or envious ignorants.

This Poet's boy offered him a cushion at his first kneeling to Her Majesty, but he refused it, saying as followeth.

THE POET TO HIS BOY, OFFERING HIM A CUSHION

Non iam pulvillis opus est, sed corde sereno:
nam plusquam solitis istic advolvimur aris.

108–9. where (to ... places;] Q2; *not in Q1*.

---

109. *near ten ... places*] For the large number of people who witnessed the royal progress, see pp. 2–3.

111. *heroical verse*] Latin hexameters (a metre associated with elevated subjects). The corresponding English metre (iambic pentameter) is used for the translation at lines 194–260.

111–12. veridicus vates] The Latin phrase is glossed in the words that follow (*soothsaying* = truth-telling, or prophetic).

115. *Apollo*] god of poetry and music, conventionally depicted crowned with a laurel wreath (hence *a laurel garland on his head*, lines 114–15).

117. *abode*] foretell.

117–18. *booted ... cothurnatus*] wearing the high boots associated with classical tragedy, to denote his status as a lofty poet (*cothurnatus* = of the high Grecian boot).

118–19. *as poets ... ignorants*] The comment alludes to the sixteenth-century debate over the status of poetry, addressed, for example, in Sir Philip Sidney's *An Apologie for Poetrie*.

123–89.] Though unattributed in the contemporary witnesses, the lines are now thought to have been composed by Thomas Watson (1557?–92), who may also be responsible for the English translation at lines 194–260 below. The following commentary notes on the Latin text primarily signal differences from the English version, while those on the English text mainly relate to the poem's content.

THE POET'S SPEECH TO HER MAJESTY 125

Nuper ad Aonium flexo dum poplite fontem
indulsi placido, Phoebi sub pectine, somno,
veridicos inter vates, quos Entheus ardor
possidet et virtus nullis offusa lituris,
talia securo cantabant carmina Musa: 130

'*Aspicis insueto tingentem lumine coelum*
Anglorum nostro maiorem nomine Nympham,
os humerosque Deae similem, dum tuta Semeri
tecta petit, qualis dilecta Philaemonis olim
cannea coelicolum subiit magalia rector? 135
Olli tu blandas humili dic ore salutes:
nos dabimus numeros, numeros dabit ipsus Apollo.
Sed metues Tantae summas attingere laudes:
nam specie Solem, Superos virtutibus aequans,
maiestate locum sacrisque timoribus implet. 140
Doctior est nobis, et nobis praesidet una:
ditior est Ponto, pontum quoque temperat una:
pulchrior est nymphis, et nymphis imperat una:
dignior est Divis, et Divos allicit una'.

En supplex adsum, Musarum numine ductus 145
et meritis, Augusta, tuis: o dulcis Elisa,
fronte serenata modicum dignare poetam,
ne mea vernantem deponant tempora laurum
et miser in cantu moriar. Se namque Semeri

125.] Q1; not in Q2.

126. flexo ... poplite] with bended knee (i.e. curled up for sleep, rather than praying).

128. vates] prophetic singer-poets, not merely *Prophets* as at line 199.

133. tuta] literally, safe (and thus reliable, loyal, trustworthy). For the richer implications of the English version of the line, see line 205n.

141, 142, 143, 144. una ... una ... una ... una] The emphatic repetition of the word *una* may be designed to evoke the name (Una) under which Elizabeth is figured in the first canto of Spenser's *Faerie Queene*, anticipating the appearance of the Queen of the Fairies herself at a later stage in the entertainment. The play on words has no counterpart in the English version of the speech.

142-4. ditior ... allicit una] The terms in which Elizabeth is celebrated here, together with the see-saw movement of the lines, anticipates the palindromatic prophesy inscribed on the 'scutcheon' with which she is presented the following day, contributing to the highly patterned nature of the entertainment as a whole (see p. 48 n. 6, and previous note).

142. ditior ... temperat una] 'She is richer than Pontus' (a rich province), 'and she alone controls the sea' (pontum). The pun is obscured in the weaker English version (line 214).

obsequiosa meis condit persona sub umbris: 150
qui fert ore preces, oculo foecundat olivam.
Officium precibus, pacem designat oliva;
affectum docet officiis, et pace quietem;
mentes affectu mulcebit, membra quiete.
Hi mores, haec vera tui persona Semeri, 155
cui laetum sine te nihil, illaetabile tecum
est nihil. En rident ad vestros omnia vultus
suaviter, immensum donec fulgoribus orbem
Elisabetha novis imples: nox invidet una,
astra sed invidiae tollunt mala signa tenebras. 160

Caetera, qua possunt, sacrae gratantur Elisae
laetitia, promptosque ferunt in gaudia vultus.
Limulus insultat per pictos hoedus agellos
passibus obtortis; et torvum bucula taurum
blanca petit; tremulus turgescit frondibus arbos, 165
graminibus pratum, generosa pampinus uva,
et tenui latices in arena dulce susurrant,
insuetumque melos: Te, te, dulcissima Princeps,
terra, polus, fluvii, plantae, pecudesque salutant:
dumque tuam cupide mirantur singula formam, 170
infixis haerent oculis, nequeuntque tuendo
expleri; solitis sed nunc liberrima curis,
in placidos abeunt animos; non semina vermes,
non cervi metuunt casses, non herba calorem,
non viscum volucres, non fruges grandinis ictum. 175

O istos, Augusta, dies, o profer in annos;
et lustrum ex annis, e lustris saecula surgant,
e saeclis aevum, nullo numerabile motu,
ut nostros dudum quotquot risere dolores
gaudia iam numerent, intabescantque videndo. 180
En, iter obiecto qua clauserat obice Livor,
virtutis famulae Charites, castrique superni
custodes Horae, blandissima numina, iunctim
iam tollunt remoras, ut arenam floribus ornent.

---

165. blanca] This ed. (paralleling milk-white at line 235 below); blanda / Qq.

151. oculo] (a) eye; (b) any point on a twig from which a bud may develop, or the bud itself (gardening term). The pun is equally effective in the English version (line 223).

163. Limulus] With sidelong glance. The vividness of the description is lost in the English version of the text (line 234).

> *Ergo age, supplicibus succede penatibus hospes,* 185
> *et nutu moderare tuo: Tibi singula parent,*
> *et nisi parerent Tibi singula, tota perirent.*
> *Dicite Io Paean, et Io ter dicite Paean,*
> *spargite flore vias, et mollem cantibus auram.*

Because all our countrymen are not Latinists, I think it not amiss to 190
set this down in English, that all may be indifferently partakers of the
Poet's meaning.

THE POET'S SPEECH TO HIS BOY OFFERING HIM A CUSHION

> Now let us use no cushions, but fair hearts:
> For now we kneel to more than usual saints. 195

THE POET'S SPEECH TO HER MAJESTY

> While at the fountain of the sacred hill,
> Under Apollo's lute I sweetly slept,
> 'Mongst Prophets full possessed with holy fury,
> And with true virtue, void of all distain, 200
> The Muses sung, and waked me with these words.

> 'Seest thou that English nymph, in face and shape
> Resembling some great goddess, and whose beams
> Do sprinkle heav'n with unacquainted light,
> Whilst she doth visit Seymour's fraudless house, 205
> As Jupiter did honour with his presence

---

201. sung] *Q1; song / Q2*.   205. whilst] *Q2; while Q1*.

188.] The line echoes the opening of Bk II of Ovid's *Ars Amatoria*, expressing overwhelming joy at securing a beloved object.

190–2.] The comment indicates that the translation was supplied for the printed edition, rather than being spoken, as assumed by Kinney (pp. 141–2), before the Queen.

195. *saints*] The term initiates the representation of the monarch as a sanctified being at work throughout the entertainments presented in the course of the visit, and intrinsic to Elizabethan court panegyric.

197. *fountain ... hill*] Aganippe, source of poetic inspiration, situated on the slopes of Mount Helicon (home of Apollo and the Muses).

198. *under Apollo's lute*] i.e. under the influence of the god of music and poetry.

200. *distain*] dishonour.

204. *unacquainted*] unfamiliar.

205. *Seymour's fraudless house*] The play on words here (*fraudless* = without guile), dependent on the sixteenth-century pronunciation of Seymour (= seemer, i.e. one presenting a false appearance) has no counterpart in the Latin text.

206–7. *Jupiter ... Philemon dwelt*] a reference to the story of Baucis and Philemon, an impoverished couple of advanced years, who welcomed Jupiter and Mercury into

The poor thatched cottage where Philemon dwelt?
See thou salute her with an humble voice;
Phoebus and we will let you lack no verses.
But dare not once aspire to touch her praise,   210
Who, like the sun for show, to gods for virtue,
Fills all with Majesty and holy fear.
More learned than ourselves, she ruleth us:
More rich than seas, she doth command the seas:
More fair than nymphs, she governs all the nymphs: 215
More worthy than the gods, she wins the gods.'
    Behold, Augusta, thy poor suppliant
Is here, at their desire, but thy desert.
O sweet Eliza, grace me with a look,
Or from my brows this laurel wreath will fall,   220
And I, unhappy, die amidst my song.
Under my person Seymour hides himself,
His mouth yields prayers, his eye the olive branch;
His prayers betoken duty, th'olive peace;
His duty argues love, his peace fair rest;   225
His love will smooth your mind, fair rest your body;

---

their dwelling when others refused them hospitality. The story is related by Ovid (*Metamorphoses*, VIII, 611–724). The implied modesty of the accommodation to be offered to the monarch is a conventional motif in Elizabethan entertainments (see line 255n.).

209. *Phoebus*] an epithet of Apollo.

210–12.] Compare the Poet's assertion in *Mitcham* that it is 'presumption in a painter to shadow kings by copies when, for majesty, they cannot be expressed when they sit for it without fear and trembling' (lines 105–7).

214. *she doth ... seas*] probably an allusion to the defeat of the Spanish Armada, still fresh in the public mind, though a reference to England's expanding mercantile operations may also be intended.

216. *wins*] wins over.

217. *Augusta*] Roman title equivalent to Imperial Highness, but also implying the female counterpart of the Emperor Augustus.

218. *their desire ... desert*] in conformity with their [the Muses'] wishes, but also because of what is due to you through your own merit.

219. *Eliza*] one of a number of names under which the monarch was celebrated in literary effusions (see also lines 399, 409, and 428).

222. *Under my ... himself*] i.e. the Poet, with all his accoutrements, is a projection of Hertford himself.

223. *eye*] For the pun (organ of sight / bud) here, common to both Latin and English versions and applicable in both languages, see line 151n.

225. *argues*] betokens.

This is your Seymour's heart and quality,
To whom all things are joys while thou art present,
To whom nothing is pleasing in thine absence.
Behold on thee how each thing sweetly smiles   230
To see thy brightness glad our hemisphere;
Night only envies, whom fair stars do cross,
All other creatures strive to show their joys.
　　The crooked-winding kid trips o'er the lawns;
The milk-white heifer wantons with the bull;   235
The trees show pleasure with their quivering leaves;
The meadow with new grass; the vine with grapes;
The running brooks with sweet and silver sound.
Thee, thee (sweet Princess) heav'n, and earth, and floods,
And plants, and beasts, salute with one accord: 240
And while they gaze on thy perfections
Their eyes' desire is never satisfied.
Thy presence frees each thing that lived in doubt:
No seeds now fear the biting of the worm,
Nor deer the toils, nor grass the parching heat,   245
Nor birds the snare, nor corn the storm of hail.
O Empress, O draw forth these days to years,
Years to an age, ages to eternity,
That such as lately joyed to see our sorrows
May sorrow now to see our perfect joys.   250

　　Behold where all the Graces, Virtue's maids,
And light-foot Hours, the guardians of heaven's gate.

---

227. *quality*] nature, disposition.
232. *whom*] i.e. Night.
cross] thwart (in its desire to obscure the brightness of the monarch).
234. *lawns*] meadows.
239. *floods*] waters.
244–6. *No seeds ... hail*] Though differing in detail, the 'Nature at Peace' topos deployed here may look back to lines 21ff. of Virgil's Fourth Eclogue, also inspired by Apollo and the Muses.
245. *toils*] hunters' nets.
249–50. *such as ... joys*] a further allusion to the conflict with Spain (see line 214 above), and the Catholic faction in England supporting the overthrow of the monarch.
251. *the Graces*] Aglaia (the brilliant), Euphrosyne (she who rejoices the heart), and Thalia (she who brought forth flowers), part of the retinue of Aphrodite (goddess of love and beauty). Their exquisite beauty and smiling presence was productive of joy.
252. *light-foot*] epithet denoting both the swiftness of the passage of time and the gracefulness of the performers.
the guardians ... gate] i.e. those signalling the passage from the mortal to the immortal sphere.

THE ENTERTAINMENT AT ELVETHAM

With joined forces do remove those blocks,
Which Envy laid in Majesty's highway.

Come therefore, come under our humble roof, 255
And with a beck command what it contains:
For all is thine; each part obeys thy will;
Did not each part obey, the whole should perish.

Sing songs fair nymphs, sing sweet triumphal songs,
Fill ways with flowers, and th'air with harmony. 260

While the Poet was pronouncing this oration, six virgins were behind him, busily removing blocks out of Her Majesty's way, which blocks were supposed to be laid there by the person of Envy, whose condition is to envy at every good thing, but specially to malice the proceedings of Virtue, and the glory of true Majesty. Three of these virgins repre- 265 sented the three Graces and the other three the Hours, which by the poets are feigned to be the guardians of heaven gates. They were all attired in gowns of taffeta sarcenet of divers colours, with flowery garlands on their heads, and baskets full of sweet herbs and flowers upon their arms. When the Poet's speech was happily ended, and in a 270 scroll delivered to Her Majesty (for such was her gracious acceptance that she deigned to receive it with her own hand) then these six virgins, after performance of their humble reverence to Her Highness, walked on before her towards the house, strewing the way with flowers, and singing a sweet song of six parts to this ditty which followeth. 275

THE SONG SUNG BY THE GRACES AND THE HOURS AT HER MAJESTY'S FIRST ARRIVAL

With fragrant flowers we strew the way
And make this our chief holiday.

---

264. specially] Q2; especially Q1.   276–7] Q2; The Dittie of the six Virgins song. Q1.

---

255. *our humble roof*] For comparable self-deprecatory assertions of the modest nature of the host's residence, see the Dairymaid's insistence at Harefield that 'yonder house ... is but a Pigeon-house, which is very little if it were finisht, and yet very little of it is finisht' (quoted from Bond, i, p. 492, lines 7–9), and the Angler's alarm at Chiswick that the Queen proposes to visit his master's 'shed' (see *Chiswick*, line 3).
256. *beck*] mute signal (e.g. gesture or nod).
264. *envy at*] bear ill-will towards.
malice] resent.
268. *taffeta sarcenet*] lustrous soft silk fabric.
270. *happily*] successfully.
278–93.] The song was subsequently published (with textual variants) in *England's Helicon* (1600), where it is attributed to Thomas Watson (see lines 123–89n. above).

> Although this clime were blessed of yore, 280
> Yet never was it proud before.
> O beauteous Queen of second Troy,
> Accept of our unfeigned joy.
>
> Now air is sweeter than the balm,
> And Satyrs sing about the palm. 285
> Now earth in colours newly dight,
> Yields perfect sign of her delight.
> O beauteous Queen &c.
>
> Now birds record sweet harmony,
> And trees do whisper melody. 290
> Now everything that Nature breeds,
> Doth deck itself in pleasant weeds.
> O beauteous Queen &.

This song ended with Her Majesty's entrance into the house; and when Her Majesty alighted from horseback at the hall door, the Count- 295 ess of Hertford, accompanied with divers honourable ladies and gentlewomen, most humbly on her knees welcomed Her Highness to that place, who, most graciously embracing her, took her up, and kissed her, using many comfortable and princely speeches, as well to her as to the

---

280. Although] Q2; *For though* / Q1.   281. never was it] Q2; *was it never* / Q1.
284. air] Q2; *th'ayre* / Q1.   the] Q2; *sweet* / Q1.   285. sing] Q2; *daunce* / Q1.
286. in colours] Q2; *with verdure* / Q1.   287. Yields] Q2; *Gives* / Q1.   289. sweet] Q2; *new* / Q1.   290. whisper] Q2; *whistle* / Q1.   292. deck] Q2; *clad* / Q1.
295. when] Nichols; *not in* Qq.   295–301. Her majesty ... into the house] Q2; *not in* Q1.

---

280. *clime*] region, realm.
282. *second Troy*] an allusion to the legend that Brutus, a grandson of Aeneas, founded London, which he named Troynovant, in memory of his ancestral home.
284. *balm*] a legendary medicament, noted for its fragrance and soothing properties.
285. *Satyrs*] exuberant mythological beings, half man, half goat, associated with the vital powers of nature.
286. *dight*] dressed.
289. *record*] sing, pipe (cf. modern English 'recorder').
292. *deck*] dress.
weeds] garments.
295–6. *Countess of Hertford*] Frances Howard, daughter of Lord Howard of Effingham.
299. *comfortable*] supportive, reassuring.

THE ENTERTAINMENT AT ELVETHAM 71

Earl of Hertford standing hard by, to the great rejoicing of many 300
beholders. And after Her Majesty's entrance into the house, where she
had not rested her a quarter of an hour, but from the Snail Mount and
the Ship Isle in the pond (both being near under the prospect of her
gallery window) there was a long volley of chambers, and two brass
pieces discharged. After this, supper was served in, first to Her Majesty, 305
and then to the nobles and others. Were it not that I would not seem
to flatter the honourable-minded Earl, or but that I fear to displease
him (who rather desired to express his loyal duty in his liberal bounty
than to hear of it again) I could here willingly particulate the store of
his cheer and provision, as likewise the careful and kind diligence of 310
his servants, expressed in their quiet service to Her Majesty and the
nobility, and by their loving entertainment to all other, friends or strangers. But I leave the bounty of the one and the industry of the others to
the just report of such as beheld or tasted the plentiful abundance of
that time and place. 315

After supper was ended, Her Majesty graciously admitted unto her
presence a notable consort of six musicians, which the Earl of Hertford
had provided to entertain Her Majesty withal at her good will and
pleasure, and when it should seem good to Her Highness. Their music
so highly pleased her, that in grace and favour thereof she gave a new 320
name unto one of their pavans, made long since by Master Thomas
Morley, then organist of Paul's church.

These are the chief points which I noted in the first day's entertainment. Now therefore it followeth that I proceed to the second.

304–5. *and two brass pieces*] Q2; *not in Q1*.   318. *good will*] Q2; *will Q1*.

---

303. *under the prospect*] within view.
304. *chambers*] small pieces of ordnance, used to fire salutes.
305. *pieces*] cannon.
supper] See line 90n.
309. *hear of it again*] have it rehearsed.
particulate] detail.
309–10. *store of his cheer*] hospitable abundance of his fare.
310. *kind*] dutiful.
312. *loving*] caring, warm.
317. *notable consort ... musicians*] Davies notes that 'Presumably this was the same mixed consort of six instruments that was to accompany both the Fairies' song and the "Come again" duet on the Thursday morning, and was to perform during dinner on Tuesday' (Nichols, iii, p. 580n.). *consort* = company of musicians. The term recurs at line 739.
321. *pavans*] type of slow-paced music designed to accompany a stately dance form.
321–2.] *Thomas Morley ... church*] celebrated sixteenth-century composer (1557?–1602). This is the earliest known reference to his appointment as organist at St Paul's cathedral.

THE SECOND DAY'S ENTERTAINMENT

On the next day following, being Tuesday and Saint Matthew's festival, there was in the morning presented to Her Majesty a fair and rich gift from the Countess of Hertford, which greatly pleased and contented Her Highness. The forenoon was so wet and stormy that nothing of pleasure could be presented to Her Majesty. Yet it held up a little before dinner time, and all the day after, where otherwise fair sports would have been buried in foul weather.

This day, Her Majesty dined, with her nobles about her, in the Room of Estate, new-builded on the hillside above the pond's head. There sat below her many lords, ladies and knights. And as Her Majesty sat at dinner, there was a door set wide open for air, whereby the people might (to their great comfort) behold Her Majesty's presence in open view. The manner of service and abundance of dainties I omit, upon just consideration, as also the ordnance discharged in the beginning of dinner, and variety of consorted music all dinner time.

Presently after dinner, the Earl of Hertford caused a large canopy of estate to be set at the pond's head for Her Majesty to sit under, and to view some sports prepared in the water. The canopy was of green satin, lined with green taffeta sarcenet, every seam covered with a broad silver lace; valenced about, and fringed with green silk and silver more than a handbreadth in depth; supported with four silvered pillars movable, and decked above head with four white plumes, spangled with silver. This canopy being upheld by four worthy knights – Sir Henry Grey, Sir Walter Hungerford, Sir James Marvyn, and Sir George Carey – and

---

327–9. there was ... Highness] Q2; *not in* Q1.   335–7. And as ... open view] Q2; *not in* Q1.   340. and variety ... time] Q2; *not in* Q1.   346. silvered] Q2; siluer Q1.   348–9. worthy knights ... Carey] Q2 *(subst.);* of my Lordes chiefe Gentlemen Q1.

---

326. *Saint Matthew's festival*] i.e. the feast day of St Matthew (21 September).
329. *forenoon*] morning.
330. *held up*] eased, stopped raining.
331. *dinner time*] i.e. circa twelve o'clock.
338–9. *upon just consideration*] after careful thought.
341. *Presently*] soon.
341–2. *canopy of estate*] ornate canopy traditionally positioned above the monarch's throne (here, the place of honour at the head of the lake).
344. *taffeta sarcenet*] See line 268n.
345. *valenced about*] with a draped edging.
347. *decked*] decorated.
348. *Sir Henry Grey*] prominent courtier, cousin of Katherine Grey, Hertford's first wife (see p. 47).
348–9. *Sir Walter Hungerford*] Known as 'the Knight of Farley', Hungerford was renowned for his prowess in a variety of sports.
349. *Sir James Marvyn*] an Esquire of the Body (personal attendant of the sovereign), knighted in 1574.
Sir George Carey] A second cousin of the monarch, Carey oversaw the defence of the Isle of Wight against the Spanish Armada and was appointed Lord Chamberlain in 1597.

tapestry spread all about the pond's head, Her Majesty, about four of the clock, came and sat under it, to expect the issue of some device, being advertised that there was some such thing towards.

At the further end of the pond there was a bower, close built to the brink thereof, out of which there went a pompous array of sea-persons, which waded breast-high, or swam, till they approached near the seat of Her Majesty. Nereus, the prophet of the sea, attired in red silk and having a four-cornered cap on his curled head, did swim before the rest as their pastor and guide. After him came five Tritons, breast-high in the water, all with grizzly heads and beards of divers colours and fashions, and all five cheerfully sounding their trumpets. After them went two other gods of the sea, Neptune and Oceanus, and after them Phorcus and Glaucus, leading between them that pinnace whereof I spake in the beginning of this treatise.

In the pinnace were three virgins, which, with their cornets, played Scottish jigs, made three parts in one. There was also in the said pinnace another nymph of the sea, named Neaera, the old supposed love of Sylvanus, a god of the woods. Near to her were placed three excellent

---

357. *four*] Q2; *not in Q1*. 361–2. *and after ... Glaucus*] *not in Q1*.

---

351. *to expect ... device*] in expectation of some ensuing entertainment.
352. *being advertised*] having been given notice.
towards] in hand, about to take place.
354. *pompous array*] stately parade.
356. *Nereus*] See Proem, line 67n.
356–7. *attired in ... cap*] i.e. dressed as a Doctor of Divinity (i.e. in visual signifiers of his insight).
358. *pastor*] shepherd (i.e. their leader and guide, in both a literal and a spiritual sense).
Tritons] sons of Poseidon, half men, half fish, conventionally depicted with conches (large seashells, used as trumpets), blown to calm the waves at their father's command.
359. *grizzly*] grey, grizzled (*heads* = hair).
360. *trumpets*] i.e. conches (see line 358n).
361. *Neptune*] Roman equivalent of Poseidon.
Oceanus] Greek god of the waters thought to surround the entirety of the earth.
362. *Phorcus*] sea deity described by Homer as 'the old man of the sea'.
Glaucus] a fisherman and boat-builder, transformed into a marine deity after the sea fight between Jason (for whom he had built the *Argo*) and the Tyrrhenians.
pinnace] See Proem, line 58n.
364. *cornets*] i.e. cornetti, rather than modern cornets. Davies notes, 'woodwind instruments, recorder-like with finger-holes but sounded through a cupped mouthpiece in the manner of brass instruments' (Nichols, iii, p. 582n.).
365. *Scottish jigs*] characterized by Shakespeare as 'hot ... hasty ... [and] fantastical' (*MA*, 2.1.68–9).
three parts in one] i.e. with three performers, the second and third precisely echoing the first in the manner of a canon or round.
366. *old supposed*] imagined to be the former.
367. *Sylvanus*] See Proem, line 76n.

voices, to sing to one lute, and in two other boats hard by other lutes and voices to answer by manner of echo. After the pinnace and two other boats, which were drawn after it by other sea gods, the rest of the train followed, breast-high in the water, all attired in ugly marine suits, and every one armed with a huge wooden squirt in his hand, to what end it shall appear hereafter. In their marching towards the pond, all along the middle of the current, the Tritons sounded one half of the way, and then they ceasing the cornets played their Scottish jigs. The melody was sweet, and the show stately.

By the way, it is needful to touch here many things abruptly, for the better understanding of that which followeth. First, that in the pinnace are two jewels to be presented Her Majesty, the one by Nereus, the other by Neaera. Secondly, that the Fort in the pond is round environed with armed men. Thirdly, that the Snail Mount now resembleth a monster, having horns of bulrushes, full of wild-fire, continually burning. And lastly, that the god Sylvanus lieth with his train not far off in the woods, and will shortly salute Her Majesty, and present her with a holy scutcheon, wherein Apollo had long since written her praises.

All this remembered and considered, I now return to the sea gods, who, having under the conduct of Nereus brought the pinnace near before Her Majesty, Nereus made his oration as followeth. But before he began, he made a privy sign unto one of his train, which was gotten up into the Ship Isle, directly before Her Majesty, and he presently did cast himself down, doing a somersault from the Isle into the water, and then swam to his company.

---

382. of bulrushes] Q2; *not in* Q1.

---

371. *ugly*] grotesque (also at line 524).
372. *squirt*] portable device for squirting water.
374. *sounded*] blew their trumpets.
377. *abruptly*] in brief.
380. *Fort*] Neptune's fort, raised for the protection of Elizabeth herself (see line 425 below), and thus suggestive of England, guarded by land (*round environed with armed men*: line 380-1) and sea (represented by the lake).
round environed] encircled.
381. *Snail Mount*] representative of the slow-moving Spanish Armada (see lines 419-22).
382. *wild-fire*] inflammable substance used in warfare, readily ignited but hard to extinguish (hence *continually burning*).
383. *train*] followers.
385. *scutcheon*] shield, conventionally bearing a heraldic device.
Apollo] See line 115n.
390. *privy*] secret.
391. *Ship Isle*] construed by Nereus as the vessel that brought India to England (lines 410-18).

THE ENTERTAINMENT AT ELVETHAM

THE ORATION OF NEREUS TO HER MAJESTY

Fair Cynthia, the wide Ocean's Empress, 395
I, watery Nereus, hovered on the coast
To greet Your Majesty with this my train
Of dancing Tritons and shrill singing Nymphs.
But all in vain, Eliza was not there,
For which our Neptune grieved, and blamed the star 400
Whose thwarting influence dashed our longing hope.
Therefore, impatient that this worthless earth
Should bear Your Highness' weight, and we sea gods,
Whose jealous waves have swallowed up your foes,
And to your realm are walls impregnable, 405
With such large favour seldom time are graced,
I from the deeps have drawn this winding flood,
Whose crescent form figures the rich increase
Of all that sweet Eliza holdeth dear.
And with me came gold-breasted India, 410
Who, daunted at your sight, leaped to the shore,
And sprinkling endless treasure on this Isle,
Left me this jewel to present Your Grace,
For him that, under you, doth hold this place.
See where her ship remains whose silk-woven tackling 415
Is turned to twigs, and threefold mast to trees,
Receiving life from verdure of your looks,
For what cannot your gracious looks effect?
Yon ugly monster, creeping from the south
To spoil these blessed fields of Albion, 420

---

419. Yon] *Q1*; *You* / *Q2*.

---

395. *Cynthia*] surname of Diana, goddess of the moon. The name was frequently applied to Elizabeth in sixteenth-century court panegyric (cf. Lyly's *Endymion*), signifying her aloofness, chastity, governance of the seas, and pervasive influence over human affairs. The crescent shape of the lake functions as a visual signifier of the name.
400. *star*] fate.
402. *worthless earth*] i.e. as against the deserving seas.
404. *Whose jealous ... foes*] a reference to the adverse sailing conditions that contributed to the defeat of the Spanish Armada.
407. *this winding flood*] i.e. the crescent-shaped lake.
409. *crescent form*] waxing shape (implying the *rich increase* to come).
410. *India*] i.e. the West Indies, noted for the wealth their discovery brought to the old world. Hence *gold-breasted*.
414. *him that ... place*] i.e. Edward Seymour himself.
417. *verdure of your looks*] your growth-endowing glance (*verdure* = lush greenness).
419. *ugly monster*] i.e. the Snail Mount, representative of the Spanish Armada.
420. *spoil*] despoil, ravage.
Albion] ancient name for England, possibly deriving from the white cliffs of the south-east coast.

By self-same beams is changed into a snail,
Whose bulrush horns are not of force to hurt.
As this snail is, so be thine enemies,
And never yet did Nereus wish in vain.
That fort did Neptune raise for your defence,   425
And in this barque, which gods hale near the shore,
White-footed Thetis sends her music-maids
To please Eliza's ears with harmony.
Hear them, fair Queen, and when their music ends,
My Tritons shall awake the sylvan gods,   430
To do their homage to Your Majesty.

This oration being delivered, and withal the present whereof he spake, which was hidden in a purse of green rushes cunningly woven together, immediately the three voices in the pinnace sung a song to the lute with excellent divisions, and the end of every verse was replied by   435
lutes and voices in the other boat somewhat afar off, as if they had been echoes.

THE SONG PRESENTED BY NEREUS ON THE WATER, SUNG DIALOGUE-WISE, EVERY FOURTH VERSE ANSWERED WITH TWO ECHOES   440

Demand. How haps it now, when prime is done,
          Another spring time is begun?

---

430. Tritons] Nichols; Triton / Qq.   438–65.] Q2; The Sea nymphes Dittie. / *How haps that now, when prime is don, / An other spring time is begun? / Our hemisphere is ouerrunne, / With beauty of a second Sunne. / Eccho. A second Sun. / What second Sun hath raies so bright, / To cause this vnacquainted light? / Tis faire* Elisaes *matchlesse Grace, / Who with her beames doth blesse the place, / Eccho. Doth blesse the place. / Q1.*

---

422. *bulrush*] water plant, formidable in its nominal associations and the height and shape of its stems, but proverbially weak (Tilley, B709).
425. *That fort*] i.e. the third of three artificial islands in the lake.
426. *barque*] boat.
hale] draw.
427. *Thetis*] a daughter of Nereus and Doris, described by Homer as 'silver-footed'.
430. *sylvan*] woodland.
432. *withal*] also, with it.
433. *cunningly*] skilfully.
435. *excellent divisions*] the adroit execution of rapid melodic passages (originally through the division of a succession of long notes into several short ones). Compare Mitcham, line 184. The term recurs at *Elvetham*, line 740.
439. VERSE] line.
441. *haps it*] does it happen.
prime] spring.

Respond. Our happy soil is overrun,
    With beauty of a second sun.
        Echo. A second sun.   445

Demand. What heavenly lamp with holy light,
    Doth so increase our clime's delight?
Respond. A lamp whose beams are ever bright,
    And never fears approaching night.
        Echo. Approaching night.   450

Demand. Why sing we not eternal praise,
    To that fair shine of lasting days?
Respond. He shames himself that once assays,
    To fold such wonder in sweet lays.
        Echo. In sweet lays.   455

Demand. O yet, devoid of envious blame,
    Thou mayst unfold her sacred name.
Respond. 'Tis dread Eliza, that fair Dame,
    Who fills the golden trump of Fame.
        Echo. Trump of fame.   460

Demand. O never may so sweet a Queen
    See dismal days or deadly teen.
Repond. Grant heavens her days may still be green,
    For like to her was never seen.
        Echo. Was never seen.   465

  This song being ended, Nereus commanded the five Tritons to sound. Then came Sylvanus with his attendants from the wood: himself attired from the middle downwards to the knee in kids' skins, with the hair on; his legs, body, and face naked, but dyed over with saffron; and his

---

  453–4. *He shames ... lays*] Compare the repeated assertion in *Mitcham* that the arts are unequal to capturing the wonder of Elizabeth. *lays* = narrative poems intended to be sung.
  458. *dread*] revered.
  459. *golden trump of Fame*] Fama, the Roman goddess of reputation, was frequently depicted with two trumpets, one of gold, which proclaimed virtue, the other black, which spread malicious rumour.
  462. *teen*] grief.
  463. *be green*] flourish (cf. line 417).
  466. *sound*] blow their trumpets.
  Sylvanus] See 'Proem', line 76n.
  469. *saffron*] yellow dye made from the stigma of the autumn crocus.

head hooded with a goat's skin, and two little horns over his forehead; bearing in his right hand an olive tree, and in his left a scutcheon whereof I spake somewhat before. His followers were all covered with ivy leaves, and bare in their hands boughs, made like darts. At their approach near Her Majesty, Sylvanus spake as followeth, and delivered up his scutcheon engraven with golden characters, Nereus and his train still continuing near Her Highness.

THE ORATION OF SYLVANUS

> Sylvanus comes from out the leafy groves
> To honour her whom all the world adores,
> Fair Cynthia, whom no sooner Nature framed,
> And decked with fortunes and with Virtue's dower,
> But straight admiring what her skill had wrought,
> She broke the mould that never sun might see
> The like to Albion's Queen for excellence.
> 'Twas not the Tritons' air-enforcing shell,
> As they perhaps would proudly make their vaunt,
> But those fair beams that shoot from Majesty,
> Which drew our eyes to wonder at thy worth.
> That worth breeds wonder, wonder holy fear,
> And holy fear unfeigned reverence.
> Amongst the wanton days of golden age,
> Apollo, playing in our pleasant shades,
> And printing oracles in every leaf,
> Let fall this sacred scutcheon from his breast,
> Wherein is writ, '*Detur dignissimae*'.
> O therefore hold what heaven hath made thy right,
> I, but in duty, yield desert her due.
>
> *Nereus.* But see, Sylvanus, where thy love doth sit.

---

474. approach] *Q2*; reproche *Q1*.   483. broke] *Q1 (broake)*; brake *Q2*.

471-2. *a scutcheon ... before*] See lines 383-6.
473. *darts*] spears.
480. *Cynthia*] See line 395n.
485. *air-enforcing shell*] conch (see line 358n.).
486. *vaunt*] boast.
491. *wanton*] carefree.
golden age] mythological first and best age of the world, characterized by peace, plenty, and harmony between species.
492. *playing*] making music.
in our ... shades] i.e. in the pleasing shade of the woods.
495. *Detur dignissimae*] 'Let it be given to the worthiest.' The inscription carries echoes of that on the golden apple presented to Aphrodite in the judgement of Paris.

THE ENTERTAINMENT AT ELVETHAM 79

Sylvanus. My sweet Neaera, was her ear so near?
   [*To Nereus*] O, set my heart's delight upon this bank,   500
   That in compassion of old sufferance,
   She may relent in sight of Beauty's Queen.
Nereus. On this condition shall she come on shore,
   That with thy hand thou plight a solemn vow
   Not to profane her undefiled state.   505
Sylvanus. Here, take my hand, and therewithal I vow –
Nereus. That water will extinguish wanton fire.

Nereus, in pronouncing this last line, did pluck Sylvanus over head and ears into the water, where all the sea gods, laughing, did insult over him. In the meanwhile, Her Majesty perused the verses written in the   510
scutcheon, which were these.

   Aoniis prior, & Diuis es pulchrior alti
   Aequoris, ac Nymphis es prior Idaliis.
   Idliis prior es Nymphis, ac aequoris alti
   Pulchrior es Diuis, & prior Aoniis.   515

Over these verses was this posy written: '*Detur dignissimae*'.
After that the sea gods had sufficiently ducked Sylvanus, they suffered him to creep to the land, where he no sooner set footing, but crying 'Revenge, revenge' he and his begun a skirmish with those of the water, the one side throwing their darts, and the other using their   520
squirts, and the Tritons sounding a point of war. At the last, Nereus

---

499. ear] *Q1*; care *Q2*. 513. Aequoris] *Q1*; Equoris / *Q2*. 515. es] *Q2*; & / *Q1*. &] *Q2*; ac / *Q1*.

---

   499. *was her ... near*] could she hear me speak.
   501. *old sufferance*] former heartache.
   504–5. *with thy ... state*] Defined by his appearance as a Satyr (see lines 467–70), Sylvanus is aligned here with ungoverned sensuality, rather than the fertility of nature. Hence the condition that Nereus imposes before (seemingly) agreeing to his request.
   507. *wanton fire*] ungoverned lust.
   509. *insult*] triumph scornfully.
   512–15.] The verses take the form of a palindrome, which may be translated as: 'You are superior to the Muses and fairer than the goddesses of the deep sea, and you are superior to the Idalian nymphs. / You are superior to the Idalian nymphs and you are fairer than the goddesses of the deep sea, and superior to the Muses'. The lines echo a palindrome inspired by Apollo in Lyly's *The Woman in the Moon* (3.1.111–15). *Idalian nymphs* = attendants of Venus.
   516. Detur dignissimae] See line 495n.
   517–18. *suffered*] permitted.
   521. *point of war*] military salute.

parted the fray with a line or two grounded on the excellence of Her
Majesty's presence, as being a friend always to peace and enemy to war.
Then Sylvanus, being so ugly, and running toward the bower at the end
of the pond, affrighted a number of the country people that they ran   525
from him for fear, and thereby moved great laughter. His followers
retired to the woods, and Neaera, his fair love in the pinnace, presenting
Her Majesty a sea jewel bearing the form of a fan, spake unto her as
followeth.

THE ORATION OF FAIR NEAERA 530

> When Neptune late bestowed on me this barque,
> And sent by me this present to Your Grace,
> Thus Nereus sung, who never sings but truth:
> 'Thine eyes, Neaera, shall in time behold
> A sea-born Queen, worthy to govern kings,   535
> On her depends the fortune of thy boat,
> If she but name it with a blissful word,
> And view it with her life-inspiring beams.
> Her beams yield gentle influence, like fair stars,
> Her silver-sounding word is prophecy.'   540
> Speak, sacred Sibyl, give some prosperous name,
> That it may dare attempt a golden fleece,
> Or dive for pearls and lay them in thy lap.
> For wind and waves, and all the world besides,
> Will make her way, whom thou shalt doom to bliss;   545
> For what is Sybil's speech but oracle?

Here Her Majesty named the pinnace the Bonadventure, and Neaera
went on with her speech as followeth.

---

523. a friend always] *Q2*; always friend *Q1*.   524–6. being so ugly ... laughter] *Q2*;
with *Q1*.   533. sung] *Q1*; song / *Q2*.

---

522. *grounded*] based.
524. *ugly*] grotesque in appearance.
539. *yield gentle ... stars*] a reference to the belief that celestial bodies govern the
lives of those on earth.
541. *Sibyl*] prophetess (specifically the figure in classical mythology consulted by
Aeneas prior to his descent into the lower world, and noted for a collection of prophe-
cies which Tarquinius declined, unwisely, to buy).
542. *dare attempt ... fleece*] i.e. have the courage to undertake an enterprise comparable to Jason's pursuit of the legendary golden fleece.
545. *make her ... bliss*] give way to her whom you destine to happiness.
547. *Bonadventure*] Good Fortune. Bond notes that 'the Earl of Cumberland commanded a Queen's ship called the "Elizabeth Bonaventur" ... against the Armada in
1588' and that 'it had been Drake's flagship in 1585' (i, p. 524).

Ay, now Neaera's barque is fortunate,
And in thy service shall employ her sail, 550
And often make return to thy avail.
O, live in endless joy, with glorious fame,
Sound trumpets, sound, in honour of her name.

Then did Nereus retire back to his bower, with all his train following him, in the self-same order as they came forth before, the Tritons sounding their trumpets one half of the way and the cornets playing the other half. And here ended the second day's pastime, to the so great liking of Her Majesty that her gracious approbation thereof was to the actors more than a double reward, and yet withal Her Highness bestowed a largesse upon them, the next day after, before she departed. 555

560

THE THIRD DAY'S ENTERTAINMENT

On Wednesday morning, about nine of the clock, as Her Majesty opened a casement of her gallery window, there were three excellent musicians, who, being disguised in ancient country attire, did greet her with a pleasant song of Corydon and Phillida, made in three parts of purpose. The song, as well for the worth of the ditty as for the aptness of the note thereto applied, it pleased Her Highness after it had been once sung to command it again, and highly to grace it with her cheerful acceptance and commendation. 565

THE THREE MEN'S SONG, SUNG THE THIRD MORNING 570
UNDER HER MAJESTY'S GALLERY WINDOW

In the merry month of May,
In a morn by break of day,
Forth I walked to the wood side,
Where as May was in his pride, 575
There I spied, all alone,

---

549. Ay, now] *Q1 (I Now); Now / Q2.* 555. the¹] *Q2; not in Q1.* 570–1.] *Q2; The Plowmans Song Q1.* 574. to] *Q2; by / Q1.* 575. his] *Q1; their Q2.*

---

551. *avail*] advantage, benefit.
557. *pastime*] entertainment.
559. *withal*] for all that.
560. *largesse*] generous reward (also at lines 694 and 733).
563. *casement*] hinged lead-light window, with shutter.
564. *ancient*] old-fashioned.
565. *Corydon and Phillida*] traditional names for pastoral figures.
565–6. *made in ... purpose*] arranged for three voices for the occasion.
566–7. *aptness ... applied*] appropriateness of the musical accompaniment.
570–97. The song was reprinted, under the title 'Phillida and Coridon', in *England's Helicon* (1600).

Phillida and Corydon.
Much good sport there was, God wot,
He would love, and she would not.
She said, never man was true, 580
He said, none was false to you.
He said, he had loved her long,
She said, love should have no wrong.
Corydon would kiss her then,
She said, maids must kiss no men, 585
Till they did for good and all.
Then she made the shepherd call
All the world to witness truth,
Never loved so true a youth.
Thus with many a pretty oath, 590
Yea and nay, faith and troth,
Such as silly shepherds use,
When they will not love abuse,
Love that had been long deluded
Was with kisses sweet concluded. 595
And Phillida with garlands gay,
Was made the Lady of the May.

The same day, after dinner, about three of the clock, ten of the Earl of Hertford's servants, all Somersetshire men, in a square green court before Her Majesty's window, did lay lines on the ground, squaring out 600 the form of a tennis court, and making a cross-line in the middle. In this square, they (being stripped out of their doublets) played five to five with the handball at board-and-cord, as they term it, to so great liking of Her Highness that she graciously deigned to behold their pastime more than an hour and an half. 605

578. good sport] Q2; *adoe* / Q1. God] Q1; got Q2. 588. world] Q2; *heavens* / Q1. 589. so true a] Q2; *a truer* / Q1. 591. faith] Q2; *and faith* / Q1. 594. that Q2; *which* / Q1. 596. garlands] Q1; *garments* / Q2. 600. lay lines ... ground] Q2; *hang vp lines* Q1.

---

578. *wot*] knows.
586. *till they ... all*] i.e. until it sealed a promise of marriage.
592. *silly*] simple.
594. *deluded*] frustrated of its end.
597. *Lady of the May*] garlanded young woman, chosen by the local community as the central figure in rural celebrations of May Day.
601. *tennis*] a high-status game at this period, played by the aristocracy and members of the royal houses of Europe.
602. *doublets*] close-fitting garments for the upper body.
to] against.
603. *board-and-cord*] possibly a game analogous to volleyball.

THE ENTERTAINMENT AT ELVETHAM 83

After supper, there were two delights presented unto Her Majesty, curious fireworks and a sumptuous banquet: the first from the three islands in the pond; the second in a low gallery in Her Majesty's privy garden. But I will first briefly speak of the fireworks.

First, there was a peal of an hundred chambers discharged from the Snail Mount, in counter whereof a like peal was discharged from the Ship Isle, and some great ordnance withal. Then was there a castle of fireworks of all sorts, which played in the Fort. Answerable to that, there was in the Snail Mount a globe of all manner of fireworks, as big as a barrel. When these were spent on either side, there were many running rockets upon lines which passed between the Snail Mount and the castle in the Fort. On either side, were many fire-wheels, pikes of pleasure, and balls of wild-fire, which burned in the water.

During the time of these fireworks in the water, there was a banquet served, all in silver and glass, into the low gallery in the garden, from a hillside fourteen score off, by two hundred of my Lord of Hertford's gentlemen, every one carrying so many dishes that the whole number amounted to a thousand. And there were, to light them in their way, an hundred torch bearers. To satisfy the curious, I will here set down some particulars in the banquet.

    Her Majesty's arms, in sugar-work.
    The several arms of all our nobility, in sugar-work.

620. silver and glass] *Q2*; glasse and siluer *Q1*.   624. an] *Q2*; a *Q1*.   624–49. To satisfy ... of all sorts.] *Q1*; *not in Q2*.

---

607. *curious*] ingenious.
banquet] elaborate dessert course.
608. *privy*] private.
610–18.] The firing between the islands, together with the other visual effects, may have been designed to recall the sea battle against the Armada, given the references to the attempted Spanish invasion in the course of the entertainment on the lake.
610. *chambers*] See line 304n.
611. *counter whereof*] answer to which.
like] corresponding.
612. *great ordnance withal*] large cannon as well.
613. *Answerable*] Corresponding.
615. *spent*] finished.
617. *fire-wheels*] probably girandolas (large horizontal wheels, mounted on poles, with fireworks attached horizontally at the spokes, causing the wheel to spin when lit). The firework was noted for its spectacular effect.
617–18. *pikes of pleasure*] possibly Roman candles, strapped to the top of poles.
618. *wild-fire*] See line 382n.
621. *fourteen score off*] 280 yards away (enabling the impressive spectacle described in the following lines).
626. *arms*] coat of arms.
sugar-work] i.e. moulded from sugar paste.

Many men and women in sugar-work, and some enforced by hand.
Castles, forts, ordnance, drummers, trumpeters, and soldiers of all sorts, in sugar-work.   630
Lions, unicorns, bears, horses, camels, bulls, rams, dogs, tigers, elephants, antelopes, dromedaries, apes, and all other beasts, in sugar-work.
Eagles, falcons, cranes, bustards, heronshaws, bitterns, pheasants, partridges, quails, larks, sparrows, pigeons, cocks, owls, and all that fly, in sugar-work.   635
Snakes, adders, vipers, frogs, toads, and all kind of worms, in sugar-work.
Mermaids, whales, dolphins, congers, sturgeons, pikes, carps, breams, and all sorts of fishes, in sugar-work.   640

All these were standing dishes of sugar-work. The self-same devices were also there, all in flat-work. Moreover, these particulars following and many such like were in flat sugar-work and cinnamon.

March-panes, grapes, oysters, mussels, cockles, periwinkles, crabs, lobsters.   645
Apples, pears, and plums of all sorts.
Preserves, succades, jellies, leaches, marmelats, pastes, comfits, of all sorts.

628–9. *enforced by hand*] handmade (rather than being formed in a mould).
633. *dromedaries*] Arabian one-humped camels, bred for riding.
635. *heronshaws*] herons.
638. *worms*] reptiles and invertebrates.
640. *congers*] eels.
642. *standing dishes*] dishes with a base or stem, allowing them to stand on the table, heightening the spectacular nature of the event.
643. *flat-work*] Davies notes: 'borrowed from embroidery, [the term] suggests designs ... painted onto the sugar dishes using sugar solutions coloured with edible dyes' (*Nichols*, iii, p. 591n.).
645. *March-panes*] highly ornate tarts made of marzipan.
648. *succades*] candied fruit.
leaches] Davies notes: 'milk-based fresh, light, sweet, and creamy confections, firm enough to be sliced' (*Nichols*, iii, p. 591n.).
marmelats] sliced candied marmalade served in the sixteenth century as a dessert. Cf. *England*: 'Euphues would die if he should not talk of love once in a day, and therefore you must give him leave after every meal to close his stomach with love as with marmalade' (p. 196).
pastes] sweet, doughy confections.
comfits] small sweets enclosed in coloured sugar.

THE FOURTH DAY'S ENTERTAINMENT

On Thursday morning, Her Majesty was no sooner ready, and at her gallery window looking into the garden, but there began three cornets to play certain fantastic dances, at the measure whereof the Fairy Queen came into the garden, dancing with her maids about her.

She brought with her a garland, made in form of an imperial crown, which in the sight of Her Majesty she fixed upon a silvered staff; and sticking the staff into the ground, spake as followeth:

THE SPEECH OF THE FAIRY QUEEN TO HER MAJESTY

> I that abide in places under ground,
> Aureola, the Queen of Fairyland,
> That every night in rings of painted flowers,
> Turn round and carol out Eliza's name,
> Hearing that Nereus and the sylvan gods
> Have lately welcomed your imperial grace,
> Opened the earth with this enchanting wand,
> To do my duty to Your Majesty,
> And humbly to salute you with this chaplet,
> Given me by Oberon, the Fairy King.
> Bright-shining Phoebe, that in human shape
> Hid'st heaven's perfection, vouchsafe t'accept it;
> And I, Aureola, beloved in heaven
> (For amorous stars fall nightly in my lap)

---

656. which in] *Q2*; within *Q1*.   silvered] *Q2*; siluer *Q1*.

---

651. *ready*] dressed.
652. *cornets*] See line 364n.
653. *fantastic*] fanciful, strange. Cf. *Comus*: 'Come, knit hands, and beat the ground / In a light fantastic round' (lines 143–4).
measure] beat.
Fairy Queen] a figure associated with Elizabeth, largely through the publication in 1590 of the first three books of Spenser's *The Faerie Queene*, dedicated to (and celebrating the virtues of) the monarch.
655. *imperial crown*] closed, domed crown, framed with arches (cf. the Tudor crown of state), signifying supreme sovereignty.
660. *Aureola*] Denoting a celestial crown associated with virginity, and carrying connotations of glory, the name serves to elevate the monarch to whom its bearer defers (cf. *To do my duty to Your Majesty* at line 666).
662. *Turn*] Dance.
carol out] sing.
667. *chaplet*] i.e. the *garland*, described at line 655.
669. *Phoebe*] a surname of Diana, goddess of the moon, and thus associated with chastity.

86   THE ENTERTAINMENT AT ELVETHAM

>   Will cause that heavens enlarge thy golden days,
>   And cut them short, that envy at thy praise.

After this speech, the Fairy Queen and her maids danced about the 675
garland, singing a song of six parts, with the music of an exquisite
consort, wherein was the lute, bandore, bass-viol, cithern, treble-viol,
and flute. And this was the fairies' song.

>   THE QUEEN OF FAIRIES' SONG, DANCED AND SUNG
>   BEFORE HER MAJESTY, THE MORNING BEFORE SHE WENT   680
>
>   Eliza is the fairest Queen,
>   That ever trod upon this green,
>   Eliza's eyes are blessed stars,
>   Inducing peace, subduing wars.
>   Eliza's hand is crystal bright,   685
>   Her words are balm, her looks are light.
>   Eliza's breast is that fair hill,
>   Where virtue dwells, and sacred skill.
>   O blessed be each day and hour,
>   Where sweet Eliza builds her bower.   690

This spectacle and music so delighted Her Majesty that she commanded to hear it sung and to be danced three times over, and called
for divers lords and ladies to behold it; and then dismissed the actors
with thanks, and with a gracious largesse, which of her exceeding goodness she bestowed upon them.   695

---

676. garland] *Q1*; Garden *Q2*.   679–80.] *Q2; not in Q1.*   691–3. commanded ... behold it] *Q2*; desired to see and hear it twise ouer *Q1*.

---

673. *enlarge*] extend.
674. *cut them short*] shorten the lives of those.
   envy at ... praise] resent the praise bestowed on you.
676. *a song of six parts*] Davies notes that the song was almost certainly composed by Edward Johnson (*Nichols*, iii, p. 593n.).
677. *consort*] See line 317n. The term recurs at line 739 below.
   bandore] lute-like instrument used as a bass to the *cithern* (see below).
   bass-viol / treble-viol] lowest and highest in pitch of a family of five, six, or seven stringed instruments, played with a bow.
   cithern] guitar-like instrument, strung with wire, and played with a plectrum.
686. *balm*] See line 284n.
688. *skill*] knowledge.
693. *divers*] a number of.
694. *largesse*] See line 560n.

It was a most extreme rain, and yet it pleased Her Majesty with great patience to behold and hear the whole action.

Within an hour after, Her Majesty departed with her nobles, from Elvetham. On the one side of her way as she passed through the park there was placed, sitting on the pond-side, Nereus and all the sea gods in their former attire; on her left hand, Sylvanus and his company. In the way before her, the three Graces and the three Hours, all of them on every side wringing their hands and showing sign of sorrow for her departure. While she beheld this dumb show, the Poet made her a short oration as followeth: 700

705

THE POET'S SPEECH AT HER MAJESTY'S DEPARTURE, HE BEING ATTIRED AS AT THE FIRST, SAVING THAT HIS CLOAK WAS NOW BLACK, AND HIS GARLAND MIXED WITH YEW BRANCHES TO SIGNIFY SORROW

O see, sweet Cynthia, how the watery gods, 710
Which joyed of late to view thy glorious beams,
At this retire do wail and wring their hands,
Distilling from their eyes salt showers of tears,
To bring in winter with their wet lament.
   For how can summer stay, when sun departs? 715

See where Sylvanus sits, and sadly mourns
To think that autumn with his withered wings
Will bring in tempest when thy beams are hence.
   For how can summer stay when sun departs?

See where those Graces, and those Hours of heaven, 720
Which at thy coming sung triumphal songs,
And smoothed the way, and strewed it with sweet flowers,
Now, if they durst, would stop it with green boughs,
Lest, by thine absence, the year's pride decay.
   For how can summer stay when sun departs? 725

696–702 SN] Q2; *not in* Q1.   707–9. HE BEING ATTIRED ... SORROW] Q2; *not in* Q1.   718. thy] Q1; the Q2.

---

700. *in their former attire*] i.e. in the costumes that they wore for the entertainment on the lake.
710–31.] The governing conceit of the speech, that winter will ensue with the sovereign's departure, is particularly appropriate given the time of year at which the visit took place, and the inclement weather in which it drew to a close (see lines 696–702 SN and 744–50 SN).
712. *retire*] departure.
723. *durst*] dared.
stop] block.

> Leaves fall, grass dies, beasts of the wood hang head,
> Birds cease to sing, and every creature wails
> To see the season alter with this change.
> For how can summer stay when sun departs?
>
> O, either stay, or soon return again, 730
> For summer's parting is the country's pain.

Then Nereus, approaching from the end of the pond to Her Majesty's coach, on his knees thanked Her Highness for her late largesse, saying as followeth.

> Thanks, gracious goddess, for thy bounteous largesse, 735
> Whose worth, although it yields us sweet content,
> Yet thy depart gives us a greater sorrow.

After this, as Her Majesty passed through the park gate, there was a consort of musicians hidden in a bower, to whose playing this ditty of 'Come Again' was sung, with excellent division, by two that were 740 cunning.

THE SONG SUNG AT THE GATE, WHEN HER MAJESTY DEPARTED

As this song was sung, Her Majesty, notwithstanding the great rain, stayed her coach and pulled off her mask, giving great thanks.

> Come again, fair Nature's treasure,
>   Whose looks yield joys exceeding measure. 745
> Come again, World's star-bright eye,
>   Whose presence beautifies the sky.
> Come again, World's chief delight,
>   Whose absence makes eternal night.
> Come again, sweet lively Sun, 750
>   When thou art gone, our joys are done.

732–37. Then Nereus ... sorrow] Q2; *not in* Q1.   742–3.] Q2; *not in* Q1.   744–50. SN] Q2; *not in* Q1.   744. Come] Q2; O come / Q1 (*also at lines* 746, 748, *and* 750). *The order of the four couplets differs in* Q1.   747. beautifies] Q2; *doth adorne* / Q1.   748. World's] Q2; *heau'ns* / Q1.   749. Whose] Q2; *Thine* / Q1.   750. lively] Q2; *beauties* / Q1.

---

731. *country's*] countryside's.

732–3. *Her Majesty's coach*] Compare the manner of the Queen's arrival, when *Her Majesty alighted from horseback* (line 295). The use of a coach at the close of the visit may have been necessitated by the inclement weather.

741. *cunning*] highly accomplished, skilled.

745. *joys exceeding measure*] immeasurable happiness.

749 SN *mask*] worn to protect the monarch's complexion when travelling, rather than to disguise her identity.

750. *lively*] life-giving.

Her Majesty was so highly pleased with this, and the rest, that she openly said to the Earl of Hertford that the beginning, process, and end of this his entertainment was so honourable that she would not forget the same. And many, and most happy years may Her Gracious Majesty continue to favour and foster him, and all others which do truly love and honour her.

FINIS.

---

753. said to the Earl] Q2; protested to my Lord Q*1*. 754–5. that she ... the same] Q2; as hereafter hee should finde the rewarde thereof in her especiall fauour Q*1*.

754. *honourable*] estimable.
758. FINIS] The end.

THE ENTERTAINMENT AT BISHAM

INTRODUCTION

The tone of the Queen's three-day visit to Bisham in 1592[1] was in striking contrast to that of her stay the previous year with Viscount Montague at Cowdray. At the time of the Queen's arrival, though technically the property of Sir Edward Hoby, Bisham Abbey was occupied by his mother, Lady Elizabeth Russell,[2] a staunchly Protestant daughter of the learned Sir Anthony Cooke (tutor to Edward VI), the highly accomplished sister-in-law of Lord Burghley, and one sufficiently intimate with the monarch to receive a personal letter of condolence from her on the death of her first husband in 1566. The Queen was consequently lodging, not with a host uncertain of his position and deeply involved in matters of state, but with a hostess confident of her social standing, and noted not for her dangerous religious affiliations but for her literary accomplishments and patronage of the arts.[3] The mood is consequently celebratory rather than earnest, the emphasis private rather than public, while the diversions presented in the course of the visit are primarily attentive to the concerns of the monarch rather than the anxieties of her host, and turn on female rather than male preoccupations – affording the account of the stay published by Joseph Barnes in 1592, *Speeches deliuered to Her Maiestie this last Progresse, at the Right Honorable the Lady Russels, at Bissam, the Right Honorable the Lorde Chandos at Sudley, at the Right Honorable the Lord Norris, at Ricorte* a particular interest for feminist criticism.

A collection of items drawn from a number of entertainments, Barnes's edition records only three interludes from *Bisham*, all devised to welcome the monarch in the final stages of her journey through the grounds rather than mounted for her amusement following her arrival at the house. All three turn on the exemplary character of the monarch and involve figures drawn from English folklore and classical myth, locating the visit in the non-naturalistic pastoral environment common to the majority of progress entertainments. Thus 'At the top of the hill going to Bisham ... a WILD MAN came forth and uttered this speech' (lines 1–2),[4] 'At the middle of the hill sat PAN and two virgins' (line 23), while 'At the bottom of the hill, entering into the house, CERES with her nymphs, in an harvest cart, met Her Majesty' (lines 129–30). All three interludes involve some species of interaction with the monarch, firmly locating her in the fictive space, not solely through her physical presence but by the music with which she is accompanied, and through which she is partly defined. The owner of the house towards which she progresses is drawn into the pastoral convention through her construction as the 'Lady of the Farm' (line 164), while the majority of those she encounters are women, associated with the fecundity of the location (cf. Ceres and her nymphs), or engaged in female pursuits (cf. Sybilla and Isabella, sewing in their samplers as they watch their sheep). The occupations and sexuality of the dramatis personae combine with the fertility of the environment in which the encounters take place, transforming the distinctly masculine world evoked in the entertainment at Cowdray into an appropriate environment for a monarch explicitly celebrated in gendered terms.

The first of the three playlets initiates a sequence of encounters in which the pre-eminence of the sovereign, constructed as a semi-divine figure with the power to transform, is established over a series of contenders. A Wild Man, alerted to the presence of a superior being by the sound of unfamiliar music in the woods, is moved to condemn the cowardice and base preoccupations of the male woodland deities (Sylvanus and Pan) he had formally respected, and finds his untamed condition converted to 'civility' (line 19) by the transcendent virtue of a being previously apprehended only in dream. The identity of the hitherto unknown authority figure, to whom he dedicates his service, is announced by the voice of Echo, who names her simply as 'She', and the word resounds through the central lines of the welcoming speech, accentuated by the use of capital letters in the 1592 edition.

The emphasis on the gender of the monarch initiated in the opening lines is heightened in the meeting that follows. Coming upon Pan in the company of two shepherdesses engaged in needlework (an occupation in which the sovereign was known to excel), the Queen becomes a spectator to a witty exchange in which the lustful advances of the god are derided, and the conduct of men roundly condemned. As the conversation turns to her projected visit, she is once again constructed as a quasi-mythical figure, superior in her chastity and dignity to classical deities (notably Jupiter and Juno), and defined as a civilizing agency, not merely through the enlargement of understanding effected by her presence but through her promotion of peace, her good governance, and advancement of the national interest abroad. The terms of the encomium serve to accentuate the relationship between the monarch and the natural abundance of the pastoral arena in which the encounter is set (cf. 'By her it is, Pan, that all our carts that thou seest are laden with corn': lines 97–8), anticipating the thrust of the device that follows, while heightening the emphasis on aspects of female potency at work throughout the interlude as a whole.

Like her meeting with the Wild Man, the Queen's encounter with the virgins and their suitor is productive of an instant transformation.

Stunned with wonder by the monarch's presence, Pan abandons his libidinous activities and devotes himself (and thus the natural world that he governs) solely to her, breaking his pipe in recognition of the superiority of the harmony by which she is attended not only to his own rustic music, but the sublime airs of Apollo, to which he had previously declined to defer.[5] The emphasis on the 'sound' that 'follows' (lines 127–8) the sovereign serves as an introduction to the last and most spectacular of the playlets, in which the arrival of a figure defined both visually and verbally as a rival monarch is similarly heralded by music. On reaching the house, the Queen encounters Ceres, attended by her nymphs (cf. the Queen and her ladies), drawn in a species of carriage, and equipped with a crown of wheat-ears symbolic of the fertility of her reign. In the song attending her arrival she announces herself as the 'Queen of heaven' (line 144), superior to all other deities, and ultimate source of the fecundity of the earth. Her hyperbolic claim that Cynthia, a conventional signifier of Elizabeth in sixteenth-century court panegyric, 'declineth, / When I appear' (lines 148–9) is instantly undermined as she meets the sovereign by the spectacular splitting of her cart, obliging her to resign her crown in acknowledgement that her deity is 'feigned' (line 159) and that 'the ornament of [her] plenty' (lines 157) rightly belongs to Elizabeth herself. In both literally and figuratively displacing her, the Queen is thus defined as the ultimate source of earthly fertility and abundance, supremely chaste in her own person, but a quasi-maternal, nurturing agency in relation to the realm as a whole.[6]

While seemingly a straightforward celebration of the virtues of the monarch in line with the conventions of sixteenth-century panegyric and devoid of any deeper intent, in fact the welcome at Bisham, like other country house entertainments, was designed with a private agenda in mind. As Davidson and Stevenson point out, the Queen's visit to Bisham is of particular interest to theatre historians, in that it constitutes the first recorded occasion 'on which English noblewomen took speaking roles in a quasi-dramatic performance' (*Progresses*, p. 208), the parts of Sybilla and Isabella having been performed by Elizabeth and Anne Russell, the daughters of Lady Russell herself. The two young women were unfortunately situated, their father having died in 1584 and their brother while still a child,[7] leaving them without the patriarchal financial support necessary to secure them husbands of an appropriate rank.[8] Alive to court politics, their mother was acutely aware that, for a well-connected, highly educated young woman, the most reliable route to advancement lay through a position as a Maid of Honour to the Queen, and the monarch's visit to Bisham afforded an excellent opportunity to exhibit her daughters' suitability for that role. The encounter between Pan and the two virgins is thus not simply a mechanism for celebrating the virtue of the Queen but a means of displaying the composure of the two young women in their sovereign's presence, their wit and intelligence, and their stance in relation to a major preoccupation of the monarch – the chastity of her attendants, and their ability to resist the blandishments of the male members of her court. Similarly, the discussion of the needlework in which the two girls are engaged is not merely a polite gesture towards a well-known interest of the sovereign but a means of exhibiting their compatibility as close companions and their skill in a pursuit regarded as proper to aristocratic women, and thus as a measure of female virtue.[9]

The discussion of the classical subjects depicted by the virgins, and of the motifs and stitches employed in their execution, is also laden with significance for a sixteenth-century spectator, supplying an index of their assured grasp of that 'quasi-linguistic medium, of a strongly gendered kind'[10] through which ideas (often of a highly political kind) could be exchanged within the constraints governing the conduct of the sixteenth-century female elite. Thus the myths depicted in the samplers display not only the girls' classical knowledge but their alignment with the cult of the Virgin Queen; the three flowers (rose, eglantine, and heart's-ease) embroidered by Isabella, announce her loyalty to the throne through their association with Elizabeth herself;[11] while her use of the intricate 'Queen's stitch' (line 73) proclaims not simply her skill as a needlewoman and knowledge of her craft, but her devotion to the monarch she seeks to serve.

While being intimate in terms of both the 'farm' environment in which they are located and the private interest they seek to promote, the three interludes are not wholly divorced from wider aesthetic and political concerns. The Wild Man's praise of the monarch, for example, draws on conventional debate topoi turning on the propriety and possibility of representing the monarch, a theme common to a number of progress entertainments (cf. *Mitcham*, p. 112), and explored in a variety of contemporary literary works (e.g. Lyly's *Euphues and His England*, pp. 332–3). Though capable of being deployed simply as a means of celebrating the transcendent character of the sovereign, the motif has resonance beyond the literary sphere in that it intersects with larger sixteenth-century anxieties regarding the dangers attendant on the visual representation of the monarch, and the consequent need for the rigorous regulation of the Queen's image by the state.[12] The Wild Man's assertion that no portrait could adequately convey the innumerable virtues of the monarch (lines 15–17), and thus by implication that all pictures must necessarily misrepresent her, may consequently be construed as an endorsement of government policy by the Queen's hostess – a coded comment on political affairs in line with early modern uses of the pastoral tradition.[13] The convention is stretched to breaking point, however, in the encounter that follows, with Sybilla's open celebration of interventions by the Elizabethan regime in continental European affairs (cf. 'One hand she stretcheth to France to weaken rebels, the other to Flanders to strengthen religion': lines 102–3), in which the use of pastoral motifs as a covert means of allusion to contemporary events gives place to a direct expression of the politico-religious affiliations of Lady Russell herself.

The close proximity between the material presented to welcome the monarch and the private concerns of the 'Lady of the Farm' has prompted considerable speculation that the *Entertainment at Bisham* was the product of Lady's Russell's own hand (see Sarah Ross, *Nichols*, iii, pp. 602–3). A highly literate woman and a poet in her own right, noted as a composer of funerary verses, she has been credited with devising another familial entertainment, the *Masque of the Muses* (1600), performed at the wedding of her daughter Anne,[14] though the evidence on which the claim is founded is capable of other interpretations.[15] The case for Lady Russell's authorship may appear, moreover, to be weakened by the apparent antagonism to theatrical performance evidenced by her fierce opposition to James Burbage's proposal to open a playhouse in the Blackfriars in 1596 and the powerful allies that she enlisted in frustrating the venture. It would be a mistake, however, to conflate opposition to the public stage, with its large rumbustious crowds and the dubious morality of those it attracted, with a Platonic objection to histrionic activity as a whole. The aristocratic entertainments performed by and for the social elite were deeply rooted in the notion of drama as an educational instrument (a concept integral, in the early sixteenth century, to Protestant thought), and had long been utilized by the intelligentsia as a diplomatic means of offering the sovereign advice. Lady Russell's opposition to the Blackfriars proposal was not exclusively based, moreover, on Puritanical grounds. She herself resided close to the proposed development, with all the noise and criminality it threatened to bring, while the church with which she was associated was equally close at hand.

The problem of authorship is further complicated by the occurrence of numerous echoes of Lyly's prose and dramatic works in all three elements of the text, prompting R. Warwick Bond in 1902 to include the piece in his collected edition of the dramatist's works.[16] Though many of Bond's attributions were subsequently discounted, the discovery of firm evidence that Lyly was, in fact, engaged in the production of court entertainments as late as 1602 (see *Chiswick*, pp. 132–4) has led to a fresh appraisal of the later phase of his career,[17] and it is not inconceivable that he played some part in the shaping of the text. Given Lyly's literary prominence at the period when *Bisham* was composed, however, and the frequency with which both his prose and dramatic works are echoed elsewhere, it is highly likely that Lady Russell herself was familiar with his work, and that the echoes (detailed in the commentary notes) bear witness to her own literary and/or theatrical experience, or have their origins in her commonplace book.

In the absence of hard evidence, the contemporary stage might offer a useful parallel in terms of the genesis of the work. In his celebration of notable sixteenth-century playwrights in his *Palladis Tamia* (1598), Francis Meres singles out Anthony Munday 'as our best plotter', i.e. one notable for the production of scenarios designed to be passed to other writers to be turned into scripts. Given the close proximity between the playlets performed at Bisham and the preoccupations of Lady Russell herself, it is not impossible that 'The Lady of the Farm' performed a somewhat similar role – that she worked in close collaboration with a professional writer, supplying the 'plot' the welcome was to follow, and overseeing the production of the script.[18]

At first sight the limited nature of the entertainment and paucity of spectacular effects might also be seen to support the proposition that a hostess careful of unnecessary expense was closely involved in the planning of the work. Jean Wilson notes, for example, that the interludes required 'little expenditure' in that 'apart from the daughters' there were just three speakers, 'possibly professionals imported for the occasion', together with 'some sort of accompaniment for Ceres's song', while spectacle was confined to 'one minor effect', the presentation of a single gift, and the 'presumably minimal' costumes required for Pan and the Wild Man.[19] The argument that thrift played a significant part in the conception of the entertainment is undermined, however, by the fact that only the welcoming speeches survive, and we consequently have no way of judging how 'imperfect' our knowledge of the work might be – as Barnes, through whose agency the text has come down to us, notes.[20] There is no evidence, moreover, that the costumes for the Wild Man and Pan (not to mention Ceres and her nymphs) were minimal, or that the splitting of Ceres' cart, timed to coincide with the appropriate point in her hubristic song, was not a highly spectacular affair. Similarly, a welcome does not afford an opportunity for the presentation of a number of gifts, and there is nothing to support the assumption that further offerings were not forthcoming as the visit progressed. Indeed, it is highly unlikely that nothing more than has come down to us was planned for the sovereign's amusement in the course of a three-day stay.

For all the uncertainties surrounding the genesis of the work, however, there can be little doubt that – whether as author, 'plotter', or mistress of the purse-strings – it was Lady Russell, with her keen eye for familial advancement, who allocated the parts.

A NOTE ON THE TEXT

A series of historical factors have precipitated a number of editions of *The Entertainment at Bisham* wholly disproportionate, at first glance, to the scale or originality of the event. The initial publication of the work by Joseph Barnes in 1592, in his *Speeches deliuered to Her Maiestie this last Progresse, at the Right Honorable the Lady Russels, at Bissam, the Right Honorable the Lorde Chandos at Sudley, at the Right Honorable the Lord Norris, at Ricorte*, was no doubt suggested, not by its peculiar interest, but by the contemporary appetite for vicarious access to the pastimes of the aristocratic elite that had prompted the publication of the *Entertainment at Cowdray* and *The Entertainment at Elvetham* the previous year, and the spate of Lyly's court comedies following the closure of the theatre at Paul's. The chance survival of the piece led to its inclusion in two early nineteenth-century publications, Samuel Egerton Brydges's *Speeches Delivered to Queen Elizabeth, on her visit to Giles Brydges, Lord Chandos, at Sudely Castle in Gloucestershire* (1815), and Nichols's collection of Elizabethan progress entertainments (1823), the former prompted by the editor's own bibliographical and genealogical interests,[21] the latter by the desire for comprehensiveness underpinning the project as a whole. Its subsequent inclusion in R. Warwick Bond's *The Complete Works of John Lyly* in 1902 was based, not on its intrinsic literary or dramatic interest, but on its usefulness in relation to the editor's argument regarding the later phase of the dramatist's career, while its appearance in the introduction to Jean Wilson's edition of *Entertainments for Elizabeth I* (1980), rather in than the main body of the text, signals its deployment for the exploration of a body of material, rather than its importance as a quasi-dramatic work.

Criticism of the piece similarly reveals its appropriation to a range of scholarly agendas. While for Bond the entertainment contributes to our understanding of the career of one of the major luminaries of the early modern stage, for later twentieth- and early twenty-first-century criticism, the centre of interest has progressively lain in its relevance to a variety of aspects of cultural studies – from the career of Lady Russell herself, through the significance of the needlework on which Sybilla and Isabella are engaged, to the evidence that the welcome provides of the active participation of aristocratic women in quasi-dramatic pastimes as early as 1592.[22]

All four post-sixteenth-century editions cited above look back directly to the initial 1592 publication of the work, and adhere to sixteenth-century spelling conventions. The present edition, by contrast, though also based on the earliest witness and cognizant of subsequent editions, conforms with twenty-first-century practice in that both spelling and punctuation have been modernized, while through line numbering has been employed throughout, in line with other items in this edition. The editorial procedures, in short, in conjunction with extensive commentary notes, are designed to allow the student or general reader to engage more readily than has hitherto been possible with a surprisingly multifaceted text that has lent itself to the service of a wide variety of private and scholarly concerns, from the desire for social advancement to the promotion of a gendered reading of the past.

NOTES

1 11–13 August.
2 Following the death of her first husband, Sir Thomas Hoby, Elizabeth married John, Lord Russell in 1574.
3 See Peter Davidson and Jane Stevenson, 'Elizabeth I's Reception at Bisham (1592): Elite Women as Writers and Devisers', in *Progresses*, pp. 207–9.
4 Compare the Queen's encounter with a Wild Man at Cowdray, lines 114ff.
5 A reference to the musical contest between Pan and Apollo in which King Midas awarded the victory to Pan, rather than Apollo, and was punished for his lack of perception by being endowed with ass's ears. The tale is related by Ovid (*Metamorphoses*, XI, 146–93).
6 A contrary reading is offered by Davidson and Stevenson, who argue that 'the need to accommodate, within the structure of a pastoral, appropriate tropes of praise for a 59-year-old Virgin Queen', leaves 'the pastoral unnaturally stranded in sterility, against the whole tendency of the genre [through a conclusion in which] *Cynthia shalbe Ceres Mistres*' (*Progresses*, pp. 219 and 220).
7 Sir Edward Hoby, owner of Bisham Abbey, was the son of Lady Russell's first husband, and thus their half-brother, rather than one responsible for promoting their interests.
8 See Patricia Phillippy, *Women, Death and Literature in Post-Reformation England* (Cambridge, 2002), p. 194.
9 Ironically, the elder of the two girls, Elizabeth, is thought to have died as a result of pricking her finger with a needle soon after the marriage of her sister in 1600 (see *Nichols*, iv, p. 124 n. 282).
10 Davidson and Stevenson, *Progresses*, p. 216.
11 See Roy Strong, *The Cult of Elizabeth* (London, 1987), pp. 68–70.
12 See Roy Strong, 'Depicting Gloriana', in Donald Stump and Susan M. Felch, eds, *Elizabeth I and Her Age* A Norton Critical Edition (New York and London, 2009), pp. 746–69.
13 Compare Spenser's use of the convention in *The Faerie Queene*.
14 See Davidson and Stevenson, *Progresses*, p. 221.
15 The claim largely rests on a letter from Rowland Whyte to Sir Robert Sidney regarding the marriage, in which Whyte notes that 'The entertainment was great and plentifull and my lady russell much commended for yt' (*Nichols*, iv, p. 125), which may well refer to the lavish nature of the event as a whole rather than to the devising of the masque itself.

16 Bond, i, pp. 472–7.
17 See Leah Scragg, 'Angling for Answers: Looking for Lyly in the 1590s', *Review of English Studies*, NS 67/279 (2015), pp. 237–49.
18 A similar hypothesis is advanced by Davidson and Stevenson, who propose that she was the 'deviser' of the text, rather than the 'author' as that term is conventionally understood (*Progresses*, pp. 216ff.).
19 Wilson, p. 47.
20 See *Nichols*, iii, p. 603, and *A Note on the Text*, below.
21 Brydges claimed to be a descendant of the Queen's host at Sudeley, and had unsuccessfully claimed the title of Lord Chandos in 1789.
22 See Davidson and Stevenson, *passim*.

THE ENTERTAINMENT AT BISHAM

AT THE TOP OF THE HILL GOING TO BISHAM, THE CORNETS SOUNDING IN THE WOODS, A WILD MAN CAME FORTH AND UTTERED THIS SPEECH.

I followed this sound as enchanted, neither knowing the reason why, nor how to be rid of it; unusual to these woods, and (I fear) to our gods prodigious. Sylvanus, whom I honour, is run into a cave; Pan, whom I envy, courting of the shepherdesses. Envy I thee, Pan? No, pity thee; an eyesore to chaste nymphs, yet still importunate. Honour thee, Sylvanus? No, contemn thee; fearful of music in the woods, yet counted the god of the woods. I, it may be more stout than wise, asked who passed that way. What he or she? None durst answer or would vouchsafe but passionate Echo, who said, 'She'. And She it is; and you are She, whom in our dreams many years we satyrs have seen, but waking could never find any such. Everyone hath told his dream and described your person; all agree in one, and set down your virtues. In this only did we differ, that some said your portraiture might be drawn, other said impossible; some thought your virtues might be numbered, most

---

1. *Bisham*] Bisham Abbey, Berkshire property, approximately 30 miles from Westminster, owned by Sir Edward Hoby, but occupied at the time of the Queen's visit by his mother, Lady Elizabeth Russell (see p. 92). As Peter Davidson and Janet Stevenson note, it was 'a very convenient stopping-place for a progress up the Thames towards Oxford, or towards the West Country' (*Progresses*, p. 214).
cornets] cornetti, rather than modern cornets (see *Elvetham*, line 364n. above).
sounding] playing.
2. WILD MAN] See *Cowdray*, line 113n.
5. *prodigious*] ominous, portentous.
Sylvanus] god of the woods.
Pan] god of flocks and shepherds in Greek mythology. Half man, half goat, he was associated with the natural world, pipe music, and lust.
6. *envy*] regard with resentment.
8. *contemn*] I scorn.
9. *stout*] brave.
10–11. *vouchsafe*] volunteer a reply.
11. *Echo*] nymph who pined away for love of the unresponsive Narcissus until only her voice (echoing the words of others) remained. Hence *passionate* in the same line.
12. *satyrs*] horned woodland deities, associated in classical mythology with Dionysus.
14–17. *In this ... was I*] See p. 95. For a more extensive treatment of the concept that the excellencies of the monarch defeated the expressive capabilities of the creative arts (a conventional motif in Elizabethan court panegyric) see *Mitcham*, lines 104–91.

said they were infinite. Infinite and impossible, of that side was I; and first in humility to salute you, most happy I. My untamed thoughts wax gentle, and I feel in myself civility; a thing hated, because not known, and unknown because I knew not you. Thus virtue tameth fierceness, beauty madness. Your Majesty on my knees will I follow, bearing this club, not as a savage, but to beat down those that are.

AT THE MIDDLE OF THE HILL SAT PAN AND TWO VIRGINS, KEEPING SHEEP AND SEWING IN THEIR SAMPLERS, WHERE HER MAJESTY STAYED AND HEARD THIS.

Pan. Pretty souls and bodies too, fair shepherdesses or sweet mistresses, you know my suit, love; my virtue, music; my power, a godhead. I cannot tickle the sheep guts of a lute, 'Bid, bid, bid' like the calling of chickens, but for a pipe that squeaketh like a pig, I am he. How do you burn time and drown beauty in pricking of clouts when you should be penning of sonnets! You are more simple than the sheep you keep, but not so gentle. I love you both, I know not which best; and you both scorn me, I know not which most. Sure I am that you are not so young as not to understand love, nor so wise as to withstand it, unless you think yourselves greater than gods, whereof I am one. How often have I brought you chestnuts for a love token, and desired but acceptance for a favour? Little did you know the mystery; that as the husk was thorny and tough, yet the meat sweet, so though my hide were rough and unkempt, yet my heart was smooth and

---

25. shepherdesses] *This ed.;* shephardisse *Barnes.*   25. mistresses] *This ed.;* Mistresse *Barnes.*

---

19. *civility*] a civilized state of mind.
22. *savage*] wild man (as against one of a cruel disposition).
23. TWO VIRGINS] Sybilla's injunction to Pan to alert their mother to the Queen's approach (lines 116–18) indicates that the parts of Sybilla and Isabella in the ensuing dialogue were played by Lady Russell's daughters (Elizabeth and Anne) whom their mother hoped to commend to the Queen's attention. Hence the ensuing emphasis on the girls' skill in needlework, a gentlewomanly pursuit, in which Elizabeth herself was known to excel (see Sarah Ross, *Nichols*, iii, pp. 604–5 n. 28.).
24. SAMPLERS] pieces of canvas embroidered with a variety of stitches and motifs to exhibit the needlewoman's skill.
26. *virtue*] particular accomplishment.
29–30. *pricking of clouts*] sewing cloth.
33–4. *Sure I am ... withstand it*] Compare the heroine's response to her lover in *Campaspe*, 'I am too young to understand your speech though old enough to withstand your device' (3.1.15–16).
37. *mystery*] hidden meaning.
38. *meat*] edible matter.
39. *hide*] skin, exterior.
unkempt] dishevelled.

loving. You are but the farmer's daughters of the dale, I the god 40
of the flocks that feed upon the hills. Though I cannot force love,
I may obedience, or else send your sheep a-wandering with my
fancies. Coyness must be revenged with curstness. But be not
aghast, sweet mice. My godhead cometh so fast upon me that
majesty had almost overrun affection. Can you love? Will you? 45
Sybilla. Alas, poor Pan, look how he looketh, sister. Fitter to draw in
a harvest wain than talk of love to chaste virgins. Would you
have us both?
Pan. Ay, for oft I have heard that two pigeons may be caught with one
bean. 50
Isabella. And two woodcocks with one springe.
Sybilla. And many dotterels with one dance.
Isabella. And all fools with one fair word. Nay, this is his meaning – as
he hath two shapes, so hath he two hearts. The one of a man,
wherewith his tongue is tipped, dissembling; the other of a beast 55
wherewith his thoughts are poisoned, lust. Men must have as
many loves as they have heart strings, and study to make an
alphabet of mistresses, from A to Y, which maketh them in the
end cry 'Ay!'. Against this, experience hath provided us a remedy;
to laugh at them when they know not what to say, and when 60
they speak not to believe them.

---

43. *curstness*] malignancy, perverse behaviour.

44. *mice*] a term of endearment. Compare Feste's request to Olivia in *TN*: 'Good my mouse of virtue, answer me' (1.5.59–60).

45. *majesty ... affection*] my power had nearly overwhelmed my love.

46. *how he looketh*] at his appearance.

47. *wain*] wagon, cart.

49–50. *two pigeons ... bean*] proverbial (Tilley, P319). Compare *England*, 'With one bean it is easy to get two pigeons' (p. 307).

51. *two woodcocks ... springe*] proverbial (Tilley, S788). Woodcocks (a variety of game bird) were proverbial for their folly (cf. Tilley, W746, 'As wise as a woodcock').

springe] snare.

52. *dotterels*] members of the plover family of birds, noted for their trusting nature and thus the ease with which they could be caught. Hence commonly used to denote old fools.

53. *all fools ... word*] proverbial (Tilley, W794).

54. *two shapes*] i.e. half man, half goat (see line 5n.).

57–8. *an alphabet ... Y*] The least used letter in English orthography, Z was not generally regarded as an intrinsic part of the alphabet. Compare Kent's angry response to Oswald's impertinence in *KL*, 'Thou whoreson zed, thou unnecessary letter' (2.2.64).

59. *Ay*] Alas.

Pan. Not for want of matter, but to know the meaning, what is wrought in this sampler?
Sybilla. The follies of the gods, who became beasts for their affections. 65
Pan. What in this?
Isabella. The honour of virgins who became goddesses for their chastity.
Pan. But what be these?
Sybilla. Men's tongues, wrought all with double stitch, but not true. 70
Pan. What these?
Isabella. Roses, eglantine, heart's-ease, wrought with Queen's stitch, and all right.
Pan. I never heard the odds between men's tongues and women's. 75 Therefore they may be both double, unless you tell me how they differ.

62–3. *Not for ... sampler*] Compare *Mother Bombie*, 1.3.130ff., in which a similar query from Candius allows Livia to display both her skill and her learning through a description of the items she has chosen to embroider.

62. *matter*] things to speak of.

64–5. *The follies ... affections*] Zeus, for example, transformed himself into a bull to ravish Europa, and a swan to mate with Leda.

67–8.] In fact, the deification of chaste mortals is not a significant motif in classical mythology. The response is probably designed as a flattering reference to the monarch, elevated to the status of a goddess in Elizabethan panegyric.

70–1.] Compare Cupid's exchange with Diana's nymphs in *Galatea*, when set by Diana to untie love knots: '*Eurota.* Why laugh you? / *Cupid.* Because it is the fairest and the falsest, done with the greatest art and least truth, with best colours and worst conceits. / *Telusa.* Who tied it? / *Cupid.* A man's tongue' (4.2.53–8).

70. *double stitch*] sewing stitch performed with a thread passed through the eye of the needle and with the two ends knotted together. Used here as an image of duplicity through a play on the word *double*.

71. *true*] truthful, to be trusted.

73. *Roses ... heart's-ease*] All flowers conventionally associated with the Queen: *Roses* as an emblem of the house of Tudor; *eglantine* (the five-petalled rose, also known as sweet briar) through its connotations of chastity and reputation as the monarch's personal flower; heart's-ease (a variety of violet also known as love-in-idleness) through its associations with constancy, and its fabled capacity to induce love. The conjunction of the flowers here has invited critical association with Oberon's account of the history of love-in-idleness and description of Titania's bower in *MND* (cf. 2.1.155–68 and 248ff.).

Queen's stitch] complex embroidery stitch, forming a diamond shape. The term is used here to enforce the connection between the flowers depicted and the sovereign herself.

74. *right*] accurately depicted and thus representative of truth.

75. *odds*] difference.

76. *double*] duplicitous.

Sybilla. Thus, women's tongues are made of the same flesh that their
   hearts are, and speak as they think: men's hearts of the flesh that
   their tongues are, and both dissemble. But, prithee, Pan, be   80
   packing. Thy words are as odious as thy sight, and we attend a
   sight which is more glorious than the sun rising.
Pan. What, doth Jupiter come this way?
Sybilla. No, but one that will make Jupiter blush as guilty of his
   unchaste jugglings, and Juno dismayed, as wounded at her   85
   majesty. What our mother hath often told us, and fame the
   whole world, cannot be concealed from thee. If it be, we will
   tell thee, which may hereafter make thee surcease thy suit for
   fear of her displeasure, and honour virginity by wondering at
   her virtues.   90
Pan. Say on, sweet soul.
Sybilla. This way cometh the Queen of this island, the wonder of the
   world, and Nature's glory, leading affections in fetters, virginity's
   slaves, embracing mildness with justice, majesty's twins. In
   whom Nature hath imprinted beauty, not art painted it; in whom   95
   wit hath bred learning, but not without labour; labour brought
   forth wisdom, but not without wonder. By her it is, Pan, that all
   our carts that thou seest are laden with corn, when in other
   countries they are filled with harness; that our horses are led
   with a whip, theirs with a lance; that our rivers flow with fish,   100
   theirs with blood; our cattle feed on pastures, they feed on pastures like cattle. One hand she stretcheth to France to weaken

---

80. are] *This ed.; not in* Barnes.

80–1. *be packing*] go away (with contemptuous connotations).
83. *Jupiter*] King of the gods, and thus glorious to behold.
85. *unchaste jugglings*] lewd deceptions (as in the amorous adventures noted at lines 64–5n.).
Juno dismayed] Queen of the gods in classical mythology, Juno was noted for her resentment at her husband's infidelities and concern with the maintenance of her station.
86–7. *fame the whole world*] i.e. what fame has told the whole world (elliptical formulation).
88. *surcease thy suit*] desist from wooing us.
93. *leading affections in fetters*] controlling amatory emotions.
93–4. *leading affections ... slaves*] Cf. *Mitcham*, 'she is a virgin, that affections wait upon her train in fetters' (lines 157–8). The lines recall the episode in *Galatea* (3.4.71ff.) when Cupid is fettered by the nymphs of Diana (goddess of chastity), and forced to do her bidding as her slave.
97–102. *By her ... like cattle*] The long peace brought to England by Elizabeth is a constant theme of sixteenth-century celebrations of the monarch (cf. Edward Hake, *A Commemoration of the most Prosperous Raigne of Our Soveraigne Elizabeth*, 1575).
99. *harness*] military equipment.
102–3. *One hand ... rebels*] A year prior to the visit to Bisham, Elizabeth had sent English forces to the support of Henri IV of France in his struggle against the Catholic League, thus weakening Catholic opposition to her own position.

106   THE ENTERTAINMENT AT BISHAM

rebels, the other to Flanders to strengthen religion; her heart to
both countries, her virtues to all. This is she at whom Envy hath
shot all her arrows, and now for anger broke her bow; on whom   105
God hath laid all his blessings, and we for joy clap our hands.
Heedless treason goeth headless, and close treachery restless.
Danger looketh pale to behold her majesty, and tyranny blusheth
to hear of her mercy. Jupiter came into the house of poor Baucis,
and she vouchsafeth to visit the bare farms of her subjects. We   110
upon our knees will entreat her to come into the valley, that our
houses may be blessed with her presence, whose hearts are filled
with quietness by her government. To her we wish as many years
as our fields have ears of corn, both infinite; and to her enemies
as many troubles as the wood hath leaves, all intolerable. [*Seeing*   115
the Queen] But whist, here she is! Run down, Pan, the hill, in
all haste, and though thou break thy neck to give our mother
warning, it is no matter.

Pan. No, give me leave to die with wondering, and trip you to your
    mother. [*To the Queen*] Here I yield all the flocks of these fields   120
    to Your Highness. Green be the grass where you tread, calm the
    water where you row; sweet the air where you breath, long the
    life that you live, happy the people that you love. This is all I
    can wish. During your abode no theft shall be in the woods, in
    the field no noise, in the valleys no spies. Myself will keep all   125
    safe. That is all I can offer. And here I break my pipe, which

---

115–16. SD] *This ed.*   120. SD] *This ed.*

---

103. *the other ... religion*] English troops, sent under the Earl of Leicester, had supported the protestant Netherlands against Spain since 1585 (cf. the death of Sir Philip Sidney, following the battle of Zutphen, in 1586).

107. *Heedless*] Reckless (usage enabling the pun on the ensuing *headless*).

headless] The significant figures beheaded for treason during this period include Mary Queen of Scots in 1587.

close] secret.

109. *Jupiter ... Baucis*] an analogy frequently employed in the context of Elizabeth's visits to her subjects. For the story of Philemon and Baucis, see *Elvetham*, lines 206–7n.

113. *quietness*] peace.

116. *whist*] hush.

116–18. *Run down ... warning*] injunction indicative that the parts of Sybilla and Isabella were played by the daughters of the Queen's host, Lady Russell herself (see pp. 94–5).

119. *trip*] step lightly (looking back to the notion of 'tripping', i.e. falling, implied in *though thou break thy neck* in line 117).

124. *abode*] stay.

125. *spies*] a reference to the numerous, largely Spanish-inspired, plots that dogged Elizabeth for much of her reign.

126–7. *here I ... me do*] The declaration refers to the story, narrated in Ovid's *Metamorphoses* (XI, 146–93), of the musical contest between Pan and Apollo, in which

THE ENTERTAINMENT AT BISHAM 107

Apollo could never make me do, and follow that sound which follows you.

AT THE BOTTOM OF THE HILL, ENTERING INTO THE HOUSE, CERES WITH HER NYMPHS, IN AN HARVEST CART, MET HER MAJESTY, HAVING A CROWN OF WHEAT EARS WITH A JEWEL, AND AFTER THIS SONG UTTERED THE SPEECH FOLLOWING. 130

[THE SONG]

Swell, Ceres now, for other gods are shrinking,
    Pomona pineth,
    Fruitless her tree. 135
    Fair Phoebus shineth,
    Only on me.

Conceit doth make me smile whilst I am thinking
    How every one doth read my story,
    How every bough on Ceres loureth, 140
    Cause heaven's plenty on me poureth,
    And they in leaves do only glory.
    All other gods of power bereaven,
    Ceres only Queen of heaven.

With robes and flowers let me be dressed. 145
    Cynthia that shineth

---

130. met] *This ed.*; meete *Barnes*.   132.1. THE SONG] *This ed.*

---

the mountain-god, Tmolus, awards the victory to Apollo, while the misguided King Midas prefers the music of Pan. While Pan remains defiant, Midas is punished for his lack of judgement by being endowed with an ass's ears. The tale, which was well known in the sixteenth century, forms one strand of the action of Lyly's *Midas*.

  129. CERES] goddess of the earth and protector of all the fruits of the earth. Hence her arrival in a *harvest cart* (line 130) and her crown of *wheat ears* (line 131).

  132.1. THE SONG] In common with a number of songs performed in the course of the Queen's progress, the piece (with textual variants) was included in *England's Helicon* (1600), where its performance at Bisham is recorded. Compare *Elvetham*, lines 278–93n.

    133. *Swell*] Glory in your predominance.
shrinking] declining.

    134. *Pomona*] Roman goddess of fruit trees, beloved of Sylvanus.

    136. *Phoebus*] an epithet of Apollo, Greek god of the sun (signifying 'the bright').

    138. *Conceit*] Imagination.

    140. *bough ... loureth*] branch frowns darkly at Ceres.

    142. *in ... glory*] rejoice only in leaves (as against fruit).

    143. *of power bereaven*] robbed of authority.

    144.] a presumptuous claim, implying the usurpation of Juno, Queen of the gods.

  146. *Cynthia*] goddess of the moon, frequently used (as here) to signify Elizabeth in sixteenth-century panegyric (cf. *Elvetham*, lines 395ff. and 395n.).

>Is not so clear.
>Cynthia declineth,
>When I appear.

>Yet in this isle she reigns as blessed, 150
>   And every one at her doth wonder,
>   And in my ears still fond fame whispers,
>   'Cynthia shall be Ceres' mistress'.
>But first my car shall rive asunder –
>   [*The cart fell into two.*]

>Help, Phoebus, help! My fall is sudden! 155
>Cynthia, Cynthia, must be sovereign.
>   [*She turned towards the Queen.*]

Greater than Ceres, receive Ceres' crown, the ornament of my plenty, the honour of your peace. Here, at Your Highness' feet, I lay down my feigned deity, which poets have honoured, truth contemned. [*She placed the crown of wheat ears at the Queen's feet.*] To Your Majesty, whom 160 the heavens have crowned with happiness, the world with wonder, birth with dignity, nature with perfection, we do all homage, accounting nothing ours but what comes from you. And this much dare we promise for the Lady of the Farm, that your presence hath added many days to her life by the infinite joys she conceives in her heart, who presents Your 165 Highness with this toy and this short prayer poured from her heart, that your days may increase in happiness, your happiness have no end, till there be no more days.

[THE END]

154.1. SD] *This ed.* 156.1. SD] *This ed.* 159–60. SD] *This ed.* 168.1. THE END] *This ed.*

---

148. *declineth*] wanes.
152. *fond*] foolish.
154.] But my chariot shall split in two before that happens (presumptuous boast undermined by the ensuing action).
157. *ornament ... plenty*] signifier of my abundance.
158. *honour ... peace*] insignia of the peace you have maintained.
159. *feigned*] assumed.
honoured] celebrated.
contemned] scorned.
164. *Lady ... Farm*] i.e. the Queen's hostess (term sustaining the pastoral conceit upon which the entertainment is based).
166. *toy*] trifle (i.e. the jewel in the crown of wheat ears, see lines 130–1).

THE ENTERTAINMENT AT MITCHAM

INTRODUCTION

The scattered documents relating to an entertainment performed at Mitcham in 1598, discovered in the mid-twentieth-century by Nellie McNeill O'Farrell among the voluminous papers of the eminent judge Sir Julius Caesar (1558–1636)[1] in the then British Museum,[2] and published by Leslie Hotson in 1953,[3] have proved of surprising interest, given their fragmentary nature, to a variety of twentieth- and twenty-first-century scholars. The longest-serving of Elizabeth's judges, noted for his relentless pursuit of self-advancement and keen eye for financial gain, Caesar found himself torn between the prestige and social opportunities afforded by hosting the monarch and the costs that her stay would inevitably entail – a division of mind aptly represented by the chance dismemberment of the records pertaining to the event.[4] Lying approximately mid-way between the palaces of Greenwich and Nonsuch, and set amidst the Surrey lavender fields, Mitcham had proved a convenient and congenial stopping place for the sovereign on several occasions prior to Caesar's acquisition of the house,[5] and he had expected to receive her a number of times before the visit finally took place. Though the Queen was gratifyingly pleased, it seems, by her reception, her host was painfully aware of the cost of her 'contentment' and the lavish gifts that the brief visit entailed, as an eighteenth-century version of his own notes regarding the event make plain:

> September 12. tuesday the Queen visited his House at Mitcham, & supp'd & lodged there, & dined there the next day. He presented her with a Gown of Cloth of siluer richly embroidered, a black network mantle with pure gold, a taffeta hat white with seueral flowers, & a jewel of gold set therein with rubies & diamonds. 'Her Majesty removed from my House after dinner the 13th of September to Nunsuch with exceeding good Contentment ... Which entertainment of her Majesty with the Charge of the former Disappointments[6] amounted to 700[li] sterling[7] besides mine own provisions, & whateuer was sent unto me by my friends'.[8]

It is not only in his private papers, moreover, that Caesar's division of feelings is revealed. The surviving records of the visit suggest that it followed the familiar pattern of progress entertainments, with a welcoming show performed prior to the monarch's arrival at the house, followed by a variety of diversions in the course of her stay.[9] Rather than being greeted by the usual laudatory address, however, deprecating the inadequacies of the host's provisions, the Queen was saluted at Mitcham by a Messenger, purporting to regret that the Master of Requests (i.e. Caesar himself) had prohibited the presentation of petitions, and declaring that he had nevertheless insinuated himself into Her Majesty's presence, trusting to her goodness of nature, in order to deliver one for her private perusal – with the earnest entreaty that she should conceal its contents from her host. In fact, the Petition (printed here as an Appendix, in that it was not designed to be heard on the day) is not a personal plea on the part of the Messenger, as the terms of his speech suggest, but a private communication from Caesar himself, stressing on the one hand the poverty that obliges him to break with the traditions attending his office and sue for support (cf. Appendix lines 8–10), and his overwhelming joy on the other at the monarch's presence. The customary welcoming show is thus transmuted into an elegant device, enabling a self-made man, shrewdly aware of the balance that the visit represented between benefit and cost, to remain aloof from the overt pursuit of royal favour, while acting as advocate in his own case.

The evidence that the documents afford of the division of feelings attendant for a prospective host upon the reception of the monarch is not the only source, however, of the peculiar interest afforded by the fragmentary records of the entertainment at Mitcham. The single surviving dramatic interlude presented in the course of the visit illustrates the embeddedness of the progress entertainments in the cultural discourse of the age, in that it is rooted in a debate common to a variety of sixteenth-century literary works. The piece involves an encounter between a Poet and a Painter, who debate the merits of their arts, and their joint confrontation with a Musician who claims precedence over them both. The encounter belongs to the contemporary pan-European *paragone* tradition, a debate form turning on a competition for superiority between representatives of the arts.[10] The form looked back, in part, to the classically derived notion of *ut pictura poesis* ('as is painting, so is poetry'), and both the debate itself and the complex of ideas associated with it inform works as varied as Sir Philip Sidney's *An Apology for Poetry*, Ben Jonson's *Timber*, and Shakespeare's *Timon of Athens*. A little-known poem, from Joseph Martyn's *New Epigrams and a Satyre* (1621), quoted by Leslie Hotson in his edition of *Mitcham* in 1953, illustrates the proximity of the *Mitcham* controversy to other examples of the genre:

Painters and Poets

Betwixt these two there lately grew dissention,
Whether of twaine, excel'd in his Inuention.
The Painter sets a good face on the matter,
Though not so true but it might seeme to flatter,

> And yet protests against it, and disgrace,
> Saying what he doth is before their face.
> The Poet (in a harsh Satyricke vaine)
> Tells him he dawbes; his own the purest straine;
> Yet yeelds to reason, and (by meerest fortune
> Meeting with me) my iudgement did impotune.
> My answer was, that Painters were confin'd
> Onely to mortall shape, and there resign'd;
> But Poets were the Oracles of Fame,
> Who long since dead, had liuing still a name;
> To them I therefore did the conquest yeeld
> Who did remaine the longest in the Field:
> Yet (gentle Reader) I refer't to thee,
> Whether of twaine shall haue priority.

The emphasis placed by the competing parties on the limitations of one another's arts permitted the ready appropriation of the debate to the services of Elizabethan court panegyric. In 'Euphues Glass for Europe', for example, the culminating section of Lyly's *Euphues and His England* (1580), the ostensible author compares his situation in attempting a verbal description of Elizabeth to that of Parrhasius, who presented a large empty picture frame to Alexander the Great, in acknowledgement of the impossibility of depicting the scale of his greatness. Similarly, at Mitcham, the controversy between the creative arts is resolved, not by an agreement in favour of one particular form, but by the recognition that all three are defective, in that none is able to capture the incomparable excellencies of the monarch they seek to portray, allowing their proponents to come together in the presentation of a gift rather than an artistic tribute doomed, by her perfection, to failure.

The deployment of the *paragone* debate is not the only evidence that the interlude affords, moreover, that the progress entertainments did not stand aloof from the artistic discourse of their age. The playlet teems with references to contemporary art works, and the circumstances of late-sixteenth-century cultural production and consumption. The joint project on which the Painter and the Poet are ostensibly engaged, for example, an illustrated chronicle of the English monarchy, was plainly suggested by the publication in 1597 of Thomas Tymme's *A Booke, containing the true portraicture of the countenances and attires of the kings of England, from William the Conqueror, unto our Soueraigne Lady Queene Elizabeth now raigning: Together with a briefe report of some of the principall acts of the same kings* ..., while the Painter's derisive allusion to the Poet's promise 'for every king to set down the years, the virtues, the life. ... all in the length of a line, and to straiten [his] conceits within a penny's compass' (lines 14–17) looks back to the celebrated achievement of the calligrapher Peter Bales, who, in 1576, inscribed the Lord's Prayer, the creed, the ten commandments, a prayer for the Queen, his motto, his name, and the date on the surface of a penny, which he presented to the Queen mounted on a ring. A passage from *Campaspe*, a court comedy by John Lyly, performed in 1583 and published in 1584 and 1591, is deployed in the Poet's derisive comments on the 'homely' nature of the Painter's productions (see lines 95–9n.), while a host of contemporary pictorial forms is evoked in his scornful references to overworked visual signifiers (lines 28ff.), murals and hangings explicated by 'unpardonable rhymes' (line 87), and the everyday products by which indigent painters were obliged to eke out their means (lines 81ff.). The Painter's riposte associates the Poet's work with the contemporary fashion for 'inkhorn terms', satirized by Shakespeare in *Love's Labour's Lost*, and provides a catalogue of the analogies conventionally used by contemporary writers in poetic effusions on female beauty (lines 52ff.). Even the tools of artistic production, and a shift in turn-of-the-century patronage, are drawn into the debate. The Poet refers, for example, to the mussel shells used by sixteenth-century painters as vessels for their paints (lines 18–19), and to the preparatory process of 'grinding colours' before work on a picture could begin (line 112), while the Painter regrets that he is now employed, not to preserve the memory of outstanding individuals, but by those entirely lacking in merit or taste (lines 197ff.), and solely concerned with the acquisition of visual indicators of enhanced social status.

It is neither the insight afforded by the *Mitcham* documents into the conflicting emotions prompted by a royal visit, however, nor the evidence that the interlude supplies of the embeddedness of the progress entertainments in the wider sixteenth-century cultural landscape, that has primarily attracted the notice of twentieth- and twenty-first-century scholars but the claim by Leslie Hotson in his 1953 edition of the text that the author was John Lyly.[11] Hotson's claim rested on a numbers of factors, including stylistic similarities with the prose works on which Lyly's reputation had initially been built,[12] the wit informing the exchanges, the use of words and expressions common throughout the Lylian corpus, and the occurrence of both direct quotations from, and echoes of, a variety of Lylian works (see notes to the text below). Hotson's position was strengthened, moreover, by the discovery, during the preparation of his edition, of another previously unknown entertainment, performed at Chiswick in 1602 (see pp. 131ff. below), which, in addition to bearing the characteristic features of Lyly's style, was explicitly attributed to him in a contemporary transcription of the text. Though the two entertainments are of comparatively minor interest in literary terms, the claim that they were authored by Lyly endowed them with major historical importance, in that virtually nothing was known about the latter phase of the dramatist's career subsequent to the closure, circa 1590, of Paul's Boys, the company for which his plays were largely composed, and it was generally assumed that his literary career had come to an end at that point.

The significance of Hotson's discovery was recognized by Kenneth Muir in his review of the *Entertainment at Mitcham* in 1954. As Muir noted, Lyly's authorship of the two works indicated that 'after he gave up writing for the stage, [he] continued to provide courtly entertainments', and that it is therefore possible 'that a number of similar pieces should be ascribed to him'.[13] The possibility had been mooted at the start of the twentieth century by R. Warwick Bond in his collected edition of Lyly's work,[14] but had failed to find general acceptance, and the question of how Lyly occupied himself between the closure of Paul's Boys and his death in 1606 had remained unresolved prior to the appearance of Hotson's edition. Nevertheless, for all the evidence adduced by Hotson, and Muir's subsequent recognition of the implications of his work, Lyly's involvement in the two entertainments was roundly discounted by George Hunter in his highly influential survey of the Lylian canon (1962),[15] and the possibility that he was indeed involved, throughout the 1590s in the production of material for the royal progress consequently remained largely unexplored until recent times.[16] The scattered documents discovered among Caesar's papers may thus be seen as of importance, not merely for the evidence that they supply with regard to the range of materials encompassed by Elizabethan progress entertainments, but for the light they may shed on the mystery surrounding the later phase of the career of one of the most influential writers for the sixteenth-century stage. The piece also has the distinction of being one of the very few progress entertainments to have been performed in recent times.[17]

A NOTE ON THE TEXT

Though the surviving documents in the British Library relating to the *Entertainment at Mitcham* have been consulted,[18] this edition is principally indebted to the groundbreaking work of Leslie Hotson, in his 1953 edition of the text, in which the dispersed papers relating to the Queen's visit to Mitcham in 1598 were brought together for the first time. The present edition differs, nevertheless, from Hotson's in a number of respects. In common with other items in this collection, spelling and punctuation have been modernized and through line numbering employed throughout, while the notes are primarily explanatory, rather than focused on authorship issues. Since the information regarding the event is based upon a number of discrete witnesses, rather than continuous printed or manuscript copy, the ordering of the material is open to question, as is the range of items to include, and the decisions taken in this volume do not always accord with Hotson's in his edition of the work. The 'Supplication' presented to the monarch by a Messenger on her arrival, for example, is printed by Hotson as a species of preface to the entertainment as a whole, anticipating the speech accompanying its presentation, and obscuring its status within the evolving event. Given that it is presented in the course of the Messenger's welcoming speech, with the earnest entreaty that the monarch should read it in private and conceal its contents from her host, it is transferred here to an Appendix, in that it was clearly not designed to be read aloud, or heard by the audience on the day. Similarly, a sixteen-line Greek song, based on a text from the *Anacreontea*, sung at some unspecified point in the visit,[19] and preserved in conjunction with an accompanying Latin version, are both printed by Hotson following the debate between the Poet, the Painter, and the Musician,[20] but are omitted from the present edition, on the grounds that it is wholly unclear at what point in the visit the song was performed, whether the Latin version formed an integral part of the entertainment or was supplied when the material was transcribed, and for whom, given the Queen's knowledge of Greek, the translation was designed.

NOTES

1 For further biographical details, see Appendix, line 5n.
2 BL Add. MS 12497, 'Legal Family, and Miscellaneous Papers and Letters', folios 233, 253–62v, and 281.
3 *Queen Elizabeth's Entertainment at Mitcham*, Yale Elizabethan Club (New Haven and London, 1953).
4 A number of the monarch's hosts were similarly divided regarding the costs and benefits of a royal stay, and were conscious that a considerable outlay was not always followed by a comparable reward. Following the Queen's visit to Harefield, for example, it was noted that 'all here are not confident that [the lavish nature of the entertainment] will procure an abolition of former unkindness' (quoted from Felicity Heal, *Progresses*, p. 60).
5 Caesar had obtained the property through his marriage to Alice Dent in 1596. Alice herself had inherited the house from her first husband, Alderman John Dent (d. 1595), whose own wealth had been acquired by unscrupulous means.
6 I.e. projected visits that failed to materialize.
7 I.e. £700, a huge sum in present-day terms.
8 BL Add. MS 4160, fol. 21 (a copy of Caesar's own account transcribed by the historian Thomas Birch (1705–66)), quoted from *Nichols*, iv, p. 64.
9 In addition to the following playlet, a song, based on a text from the *Anacreontea*, was sung, for example, in Greek (see Hotson, pp. 29ff. and p. 115 below).

10 For a more detailed discussion of the *paragone* tradition in relation to late sixteenth-century culture, see Chloe Porter, *Making and Unmaking in Early Modern English Drama: Spectators, Aesthetics and Incompletion* (Manchester, 2013), pp. 3–8.
11 Or, in Hotson's words, 'either John Lyly or the Devil' (p. 4).
12 For example, his 'characteristic mixture of alliteration, assonance, annomination, parisonic and rhetorical balance, antithesis, punning and typical tricks of allusion' (Hotson, p. 4).
13 Kenneth Muir, 'Queen Elizabeth's Entertainment at Mitcham', *Review of English Studies*, NS 5 (1954), p. 408.
14 See Bond, i, pp. 404ff.
15 *John Lyly: The Humanist as Courtier* (London, 1962), p. 84 n. 69.
16 See Leah Scragg, 'Angling for Answers: Looking for Lyly in the 1590s', *Review of English Studies*, NS 67/279 (2015), pp. 237–49.
17 The work was staged in the spring of 1952 in the grounds of the Elizabethan Club at Yale, prior to the publication of Hotson's edition.
18 See notes 2 and 8 above.
19 The note on the verso of the text (which is undated) merely states that it is 'the dite of the Greak song, before the Queens Majesty at mine howse at Mitcham', and makes no mention of the circumstances of its performance.
20 Hotson also prints an English version of the same motif (Herrick's 'The Wounded Cupid') as an aid to readers unfamiliar with both Greek and Latin (p. 30).

THE ENTERTAINMENT AT MITCHAM

THE SPEECH AT THE DELIVERING OF THE PETITION

[A MESSENGER *with a petition approaches the* QUEEN *as she draws near the house.*]

[*Messenger.*] Great Lady, your Master of Requests, either with melancholy, with joy, or business, is grown so peremptory that he hath laid penalties upon all such as shall deliver petitions. I, more confident of your gracious aspect than fearful of his command, have secretly conveyed myself into this honorable troop, in all humility offering these few lines with a wish that you would be pleased to read them ere you sleep, and ever to conceal them from him they most concern. [*He presents the petition to the Queen.*]

THE SECOND SPEECHES

[*Enter* POET *and* PAINTER, *the latter with a number of pictures.*]

Painter. Thou art the dullest poet that ever hatched invention. Better to bring forth blind whelps with haste than be seven years breeding with the camel. Didst thou not promise for every king to set

---

1.1–2. SD] *This ed.* 2. SP] *This ed.* 9–10. SD] *This ed.* 11.1. SD] *This ed.*

---

2. *Master of Requests*] judge in a minor equity court primarily dealing with cases brought by the poor. Caesar held the office from 1596 to 1606 (having been appointed extraordinary Master in 1591).
3. *peremptory*] closed to objection (legal term).
5. *gracious aspect*] favourable notice.
6. *conveyed myself*] stolen.
9–10. SD] For the text of the petition, read by the Queen in private, see Appendix, pp. 128–9.
11–217.] See pp. 111–12 for the *paragone* tradition to which the debate belongs. The interlude was clearly staged at some point after the Queen's arrival at the house.
12. *hatched invention*] gave birth to an imaginative idea.
13. *to ... haste*] proverbial for a flawed, prematurely completed design (Tilley, B425: 'The hasty bitch brings forth blind whelps'). Lyly draws on the proverb in *England* in relation to his first published work (cf. 'My first burden, coming before his time, must needs be a blind whelp': p. 156).
13–14. *seven years ... camel*] Male camels do not achieve full reproductive capability before their seventh year, while the reproductive rate of the species is proverbially slow.

down the years, the virtues, the life, as I shadowed them to life, 15
all in the length of a line, and to straiten thy conceits within a
penny's compass?

Poet. 'Tis true, Painter, and were conceits as fluent in the brainpan as
colours in thy mussel shells, or invention pinned to the fingers'
ends with the pencil, I could cast sentences as thou slubberest 20
up pictures, but in our arts are as great odds as between seeing
and understanding.

Painter. Why, what is to be seen or conceived that we cannot express,
making judgement to slide from the eye into the heart? The
virtues, the senses, the thoughts – all limned out so lively that 25
even things invisible are caught by the eye, insensible felt with
conceit.

Poet. Oh, but you lay your invention to pawn and borrow all your
credit of beasts and creatures senseless. Justice with an old pair
of scales and a wood knife, as though with one hand she should 30
weigh her wares, and with the other knock the buyer on the
knuckles. Temperance with a pint pot like a tapster; Prudence

---

16. *all in the length of a line*] each of them in a single line of verse.

16–17. *straiten ... a penny's compass*] compress your thoughts into the circumference of a penny (silver coin, just over half an inch in diameter). As Hotson noted, the remark alludes to the achievement of the calligrapher Peter Bales, who, according to Stow, 'writ within the compass of a penie, in Latine, the Lordes prayer, the Creede, the ten Commaundements, a prayer to God, a praier for the Queene, his Posie, his name, the day of the moneth, the yeere of our Lorde, and the raigne of the Queene' (quoted from Hotson, p. 40). Lyly alludes to the achievement in a petitionary letter to the Queen in 1595 (see Bond, i, p. 64).

18. *were conceits ... brainpan*] if imaginative conceptions flowed as freely in the mind.

19. *colours*] paints.

mussel shells] used in the sixteenth century as receptacles for artists' paints.

19–20. *pinned ... ends*] at the tips of the fingers.

20. *cast*] (*a*) toss out; (*b*) devise.

20–1. *slubberest up*] daub.

21. *odds*] difference.

25. *limned out so lively*] depicted so vividly.

26. *things invisible ... the eye*] abstract ideas are apprehended by visual means.

26–7. *insensible ... conceit*] beyond sensory experience grasped through an imaginative representation.

28–9. *lay your ... senseless*] exchange your own imaginative creations for lifeless second-hand images.

29–30. *Justice ... knife*] Justice was traditionally depicted with a sword in one hand and scales in the other (cf. the statue above the Old Bailey in London).

31. *wares*] goods.

32. *pot*] drinking vessel.

tapster] historically, a woman who drew beer for sale at an inn.

with a snake, which is commonly made so like an eel that many thinks Wisdom to cry grigs in the street. Then Fortitude with a log in her arms, as though she should wrestle with an oak for a wager. And thus it comes to pass that whereas in an exquisite painting there should be more understood than expressed, here is more expressed than can be understood.

Painter. Wade no further, lest where I painted thee with a laurel crown I change my copy, and turn it to a coxcomb.

Poet. I fear no shadows. If words break no bones, colours cannot. But I pray thee, why is feeling tied to a spider? Hearing to a stag? Smelling to a hound? Seeing to an eagle? Tasting to a monkey? All which makes the painter resemble to an ape.

Painter. I wonder thou wilt ask reason of reason. Do not all these excel in the sharpness of sense?

Poet. No. I know others more excellent. Thou hast thrust the winds into four corners of the map, like trumpeters sending smoke out of tobacco pipes; the thoughts like Alchemists' limbecks, distilling upwards and downwards, yet finding no end or conclusion for their falling or climbing.

Painter. If thou rip up my vanities, I will open thy veins, and make the pulse that beats so fast not to pant at all. What unchristened

---

33. *snake*] a traditional symbol of wisdom.
34. *cry grigs in the street*] be a street vendor proclaiming that she has young eels for sale.
34–5. *a log in her arms*] symbolic of the enduring of heavy labour.
39. *Wade no further*] Do not proceed with this.
laurel crown] an emblem of Apollo, and hence of one with poetic gifts.
40. *change my copy*] revise my design.
coxcomb] fool's cap.
41. *fear no shadows*] am not subject to baseless alarms. The boast turns on a play on the proverbial expression 'to be afraid of a shadow' (Tilley, S261) and the use of 'shadowing' as a synonym for drawing (see line 15 above).
words break no bones] proverbial (Tilley, W801).
colours] paints. Also at line 69.
42–3. *feeeling ... monkey*] traditional analogies used as visual signifiers in works of art (*tied* = specific).
44. *an ape*] i.e. a senseless mimic.
45. *ask reason of reason*] require an explanation for something entirely rational.
47–9. *winds in ... pipes*] The four winds were customarily represented by cartographers as human heads with distended cheeks, blowing blasts of air from their mouths at the corners of maps.
49–51. *thoughts like ... climbing*] Cf. the use of thought or speech bubbles in contemporary graphic art.
49. *limbecks*] retorts.
52. *rip up my vanities*] anatomize my follies.
53. *unchristened*] outlandish.

words have of late crept into credit with new coined poetry! Such canvassing the heavens in paper blankets, words of pistol-proof, and so far-fetched circumlocutions that it is high noon before one conceives the other meant to bid him good morrow. All the pearl taken up for women's teeth, the stars for their eyes, the coral for their lips, the ivory for their necks; which is nothing else than to patch up that with words which is most amiable by nature, as though one would express the jugging of a nightingale by the whistling of a carman. English words larded with Latin, Spanish with French, all lined with such bombast that should they but pass all in their proper language, their conceits would seem so lean as though they were in a consumption, and their phrases shake as though they had been taken with a fever. 55 60 65

Poet. Fantastical Painter, if thou didst not suck all from poetry what difference were there between painting and daubing? What would thy colours serve for, but to white-lime walls, or to paint red and green lattices? 70

---

61. jugging] *This ed.;* joucking *Hotson.*

---

54. *crept into credit ... poetry*] are now approved in freshly minted verse. The accusation (turning on a pun on coin/coinages) refers to the rage for 'inkhorn' (i.e. polysyllabic Latinate) terms among sixteenth-century writers.

55. *canvassing the heavens*] tossing the skies (i.e. tumbling the entire cosmos together).

words of pistol-proof] impenetrable terms. Hotson (p. 42 n. 58) suggests that the phrase may be designed as an allusion to the hyperbolic language of Ancient Pistol in 2H4. The compound occurs in the Shakespearian play at 2.4.114.

57. *conceives*] grasps.

58–9. *pearl ... stars ... coral ... ivory*] all conventionally deployed by writers to denote aspects of female beauty.

60. *patch up ... words*] clumsily attempt to express (or improve) by verbal means.
amiable] lovely.

61. *jugging*] onomatopoeic term for the nightingale's song. Cf. Lyly: 'What bird so sings, and yet [*sic*] does wail? / O 'tis the ravished nightingale. / Jug, jug, jug, jug, Tereu, she cries, /And still her woes at midnight rise' (*Campaspe*, 5.1.35–8).

62. *carman*] carter. Cf. 2H4: 'He heard the carmen whistle' (3.2.312–13).
larded] laden, garnished.

63. *lined ... bombast*] filled out with such crude padding (image drawn from the use of bulky lining material in tailoring).

64. *pass all ... language*] be expressed in ordinary terms.
conceits] ideas.

67. *suck*] derive (initiating the breast-feeding imagery in lines 71–3).

69. *white-lime walls*] paint walls with whitewash (customarily made of lime).

70. *lattices*] interlacing wooden laths or metal bars in window apertures, frequently painted red (in the case of taverns) or green.

Painter. If I have sucked all from the Poet, I must curse the teats that poisoned my invention; and then all the error of my art must light upon the sourness of thy milk. So that if I be a fool, thou must be the father.

Poet. I confess. And it is not rare that wise men have fools to their children, nor unknown that poetry hath two teats – the one for Apelles, the other for thee. But I will prove, by thy own confession and demonstration, such a defect in thy art that time to come may blush and would amend, and time present stand amazed because it cannot.

Painter. Nay. Let us shake hands, for by these arts we must both live.

Poet. Ay, thou mayst, as long as babies for fairs, fruit trenchers for banquets, or painted cloth after sixpence a yard be in request. That thou mayst, in country victualling houses, paint the prodigal child with a grey beard, the story of blind Toby with a swallow over his head, that all the beholders take to be a lapwing; and then grace it with such unpardonable rhymes that 'tis grown to a proverb, 'Worse than the posy in the painted cloth'. Thus thou, out of a little red ochre and oils getst a living.

---

86. take] *This ed.*; takes *Hotson.*

---

71. *sucked all*] derived everything (see line 67n. above).
72. *invention*] imaginative powers.
73. *light upon*] be attributed to.
75–6. *wise men ... children*] proverbial (Tilley, M421). Lyly draws on the same adage in *Mother Bombie* (1.1.7–9).
77. *Apelles*] The most celebrated of the Greek painters, favoured by Alexander the Great. Lyly refers to the figure on numerous occasions, most notably in *Campaspe* where he appears as Alexander's rival in love.
79. *would amend*] seek to correct it.
80. *amazed*] in a maze (i.e. stunned).
82. *babies*] dolls (commonly painted).
fruit trenchers] painted wooden platters for fruit.
83. *be in request*] are in demand.
84. *victualling houses*] eating houses, inns.
84–5. *paint the prodigal ... beard*] i.e. represent the story in such a way that its meaning is obscured (through depicting the misguided youth as an old man).
85–7. *the story ... lapwing*] another example of a misleading representation of an exemplary narrative (the apocryphal story of Tobias, blinded by the droppings from a swallow nesting under his eaves). The lapwing (associated with trickery) carried very different connotations for a sixteenth-century audience from the swallow (associated with filth).
87. *grace it ... rhymes*] Painted wall decorations were frequently furnished with explanatory verses announcing the subject, or expounding the meaning of the work.
88. *posy*] legend, explanatory verses.
89. *ochre*] a combination of clay and oxide of iron, much used in pigments.

But poetry hath a dash over the head: *Ibis Homere prae*. But to the matter. [*He looks at the Painter's handiwork.*] Hast thou drawn all these kings?
Painter. All; and I think excellent for the attire and the countenance, being a true copy of those ages counterfeiting.
Poet. In what time?
Painter. Little more than two years.
Poet. I had thought in much less than in one month.
Painter. Why? Is it so easy?
Poet. No, but because they are so homely. Otherwise, one in two years were enough. Besides, I could myself out of the chronicles have drawn, by their description, a more absolute abstract, to set down their true features. But thou imitatest a silly man of thy trade that painted the Nine Worthies by report of an old man that dreamed he saw them. But to add more to thy folly, I account it presumption in a painter to shadow kings by copies when, for majesty, they cannot be expressed when they sit for it without fear and trembling. [*He gestures to an unpainted board.*] But what board is that thou porest upon, ever pointing at it, never painting it?

---

91. SD] *This ed.*   107. SD] *This ed.*

---

90. *hath a dash over the head*] can deliver a devastating blow. Compare the Scrivener's threat in Lyly's *Mother Bombie*, to deliver 'a dash with a pen' (5.3.414).
  Ibis Homere prae] Obscure. The phrase may look back to Ovid's *Ars Amatoria*, II, 280 (*Si nihil attuleris, ibis, Homere, foras*: 'If you bring nothing Homer, out you go') or, as Hotson suggests, be a mistake for *Ibis Homero prae*; 'Thou [like a fool] will go before [or show the way to] Homer' (p. 43 n. 104).
  93. *attire and the countenance*] dress and physical appearance.
  95–9. *In what ... homely*] Compare *Campaspe*: '*Alexander*. Aurelius would in one hour colour four faces. / *Apelles*. I marvel in half an hour he did not four. / *Alexander*. Why, is it so easy? / *Apelles*. No, but he doth it so homely' (3.4.88–91). The similarity between the two passages lends considerable weight to the argument for Lyly's authorship of the Mitcham entertainment (see pp. 113–14 above).
  99. *homely*] crudely done.
  101. *absolute abstract*] perfect account.
  103. *Nine Worthies*] exemplary Biblical, historical and legendary figures (Joshua, David, Judas Maccabeus, Hector, Alexander the Great, Julius Caesar, King Arthur, Charlemagne, and Godfrey of Bouillon).
  105. *shadow ... copies*] make visual representations of kings.
  106–7. *they cannot ... trembling*] the subjects cannot be adequately depicted when they pose for their portraits because the painters are so overawed by their presence that they tremble.
  108–9. *ever pointing ... painting it*] Compare Hephestion's observation in *Campaspe* that an artist becomes so enamoured of his own work that he is 'still mending it, never ending it' (5.4.21).

Painter. It is for the Queen that now reigneth, long hath, and I hope ever shall. 110
Poet. Why hast thou been longer a-grinding colours for her than in shadowing all the rest?
Painter. Because her perfection admitteth no colouring.
Poet. I have seen many counterfeits of her. 115
Painter. Counterfeits indeed, but none current. And as hard it will be for thee to set down her virtues as for me her beauty, the one not coming within the compass of art, nor the other of imagination.
Poet. It may be thou dost but flatter her, and thyself too. 120
Painter. Then say experience flatters; envy flatters; heaven flatters; and Truth, the only heir and daughter of all times, flatters. Then say that we have had no peace these many years, no prosperity, no glory, but that we flatter ourselves as though we had. Say thou art not here to see her, but flatterest thyself as though thou wert. 125
Poet. Proceed.
Painter. One painter, by the view of fifty virgins, shadowed one Venus and one virgin, by her beauty, hath put all painters in amazement, and cannot express hers. So far hath nature outstripped art that it leaveth nothing in the mind but admiration, and 130 admiration falling itself into astonishment.
Poet. Now here's that confessed which I foretold – defect in thy art and boldness in artificers. For which I will seal thy folly with this song.

---

112. *a-grinding colours*] preparing paints. Compare *Campaspe*: 'in thy [Apelles'] shop grinding colours' (4.4.17).

114. *admitteth no colouring*] is beyond the reach of art (with a pun on *colours* in line 112).

115–16. *counterfeits ... Counterfeits*] artistic representations / fraudulent imitations, particularly in relation to coinage (looking forward to the play on *current* (see following note) in the second half of the sentence).

116. *current*] (a) valid; (b) worth anything.

118. *compass*] range (also at line 188).

120–1. *flatter her ... flatters*¹] seek to please her through over-praising / is pleasingly deceptive. The second meaning is played on in the following lines.

122. *Truth ... times*] proverbial (Tilley, T580).

127. *One painter ... Venus*] Zeuxis (fl. 424–400 BC), reputed to have assembled fifty outstandingly beautiful virgins in Sparta in order to depict Venus. Lyly uses the same story in a similar context in *England* (p. 338).

130. *admiration*] wonder.

131. *astonishment*] stunned amazement.

132. *defect in thy art*] i.e. in its inability to represent ultimate perfection (as represented by the monarch).

THE SONG.

> I cannot choose but laugh,
>   To see how painters prove,
> By vain device of apish art,
>   To paint the Queen of Love.
> Where colours and conceits
>   Would blaze the beauty forth
> Of which no eye, no art, no tongue,
>   No thought can prize the worth.

Painter. Is this all?
Poet. All.
Painter. I think thou mad'st it so short because thou wantest wit to make it longer.
Poet. No, silly man; but if thou canst find any word that may nearer express thy indiscretion, then will I take the blame. If not, to avoid circumlocutions (at which thou didst at the first cavil) 'tis better call thee fool in few words than in many. But how thinkst thou it possible to shadow her picture?
Painter. As possible as for thee to number her praises.
Poet. Yet have I the odds, for though I cannot express all her worth, yet so much I can as shall make all men wonder.
Painter. That is as much as if I should draw the forehead and never finish the face. To be possessed with this in thy head – that she is a virgin, that affections wait upon her train in fetters, that there was no virtue singular in those kings [*He gestures to the finished pictures.*] that meet not all in her to make one only absolute – and not by art in the highest strain to amplify the rareness and happiness, is as if sundry of my colours should lie in several shells, and I make no use by my art.

159–60. SD] *This ed.*

---

137. *prove*] strive.
141. *blaze ... forth*] proclaim the loveliness.
143. *prize the worth*] truly estimate the value.
146. *wit*] inventiveness.
150. *thou didst at the first cavil*] you objected at the outset.
154. *odds*] advantage.
158. *affections ... fetters*] desires follow her in chains (i.e. are subject to her will). The same phrase occurs in *Bisham* (line 93).
159. *singular in*] particular to each of.
160. *meet not*] do not come together.
161. *amplify*] expatiate upon.
162. *happiness*] good fortune.
163. *shells*] See line 19n.

Poet. I told thee; felicity is to be admired, not described.
Painter. Nay, if thou crave pardon for thy head, I may well beg pardon for my hand, being one of the head's officers.

Enter MUSICIAN.

Poet. What! Cavaliero Crochet, Monsieur de Minim, Seignior Semibreve. What brought you hither?
Musician. A poet and a painter, idol makers for idleness; the one casting fancies in a mould, the other faces. What do you here? You are excluded from the number of arts. I am one of the seven liberal sciences.
Poet. Yea, and the liberalest of them, all seven. For thou playst much, and getst little.
Musician. I should; for what is more tickling in the ear than music?
Painter. A flea.
Musician. What for melancholy more sovereign?
Poet. A sovereign.
Musician. Who breedeth more pleasure than a good musician?
Painter. A good cook.
Musician. Angels frequent musicians.
Poet. Look in thy purse, and thou wilt prove thyself a liar.
Musician. What say you to nimble division?
Painter. As of counterfeit gargling.
Musician. I can astonish the senses.

---

164. *admired*] wondered at.
165. *thy head*] the limitations of your mind.
166. *hand*] artistic skills.
172. *excluded from*] not included among.
172–3. *seven liberal sciences*] grammar, rhetoric, logic, arithmetic, geometry, music, and astronomy (the subjects seen in ancient Greece as fundamental to the education of a free person, and broadly adhered to in the early modern university system).
174. *liberalest of them*] the one that gives its services most freely.
176. *tickling*] (a) pleasing (the sense the Musician intends); (b) irritating (the meaning played on in the Painter's response).
178–9. *sovereign ... sovereign*] efficacious / gold coin worth twenty shillings in pre-decimalization English currency.
180. *breedeth*] engenders.
182. *Angels*] (a) celestial messengers (the sense the Musician intends); (b) gold coins worth ten shillings (the sense played on in the Poet's response).
184. *nimble division*] the execution of a rapid melodic passage (originally by the division of a succession of long notes into several short ones). See *Elvetham*, line 435n.
185. *counterfeit*] simulated.
186. *astonish*] stun, captivate.

Poet. So can an apoplexy. But canst thou set a note above *e la*?
Musician. It cometh not within the compass of art.
Poet. Then keep thy fiddle within thy case, for thou art just in our case. Wit, colours, nor airs can express that which we most covet, her perfection. Therefore let us all join in consort, and pray that the world may so long enjoy her as time shall the world, and that after her there be neither wit, colours, nor sounds left in the world. I'll keep my sonneting for sempsters to sing over their idle lazy stitches.
Musician. And I my notes for country tunes and London cries.
Painter. And I this board for a country mistress, who cares not how she be painted, so she be painted. Our art grows stale; for where, in elder ages, none were coloured but memorable for their virtues, to paint out imitation to posterity, now every citizen's wife that wears a taffeta kirtle and a velvet hat, and every gentlewoman that can board a pair of borders, must have her picture in the parlour. And if one hereafter ask, 'Who was this?' It was one of the companies of such a trade, or a Justice of Peace his wife, of such a shire. But it is not in us only, but in mocking of ancient monuments. For now, if one die rich he must have a tomb and an epitaph, when nothing remaineth for memory but that he died

---

187. *set a note above* e la] play a higher note than E (the highest note in the hexachord). Lyly uses the image (to express something seemingly unattainable) on a number of occasions (cf. *England*, p. 155; *Midas*, Prologue, line 8; *Mother Bombie*, 2.1.147).
189. *thy case ... case*] box for your musical instrument / predicament, situation.
190. *Wit, colours, nor airs*] i.e. neither poetry, painting, nor music (also at line 193 below).
covet] desire.
191. *consort*] harmonious agreement.
194. *sempsters*] seamstresses (needlewomen who earn their living by sewing).
195. *lazy*] (*a*) languid (in conjunction with the preceding adjective); (*b*) long looping embroidery stitch (in conjunction with the following noun).
196. *London cries*] the chantings of London street vendors.
199. *elder ages*] former times.
199–200. *coloured ... posterity*] painted except those worthy of remembrance for their good qualities, in order to offer an example for later generations to follow.
201. *taffeta kirtle ... hat*] i.e. has social pretensions.
202. *board ... borders*] afford to wear embroidered trimmings at her neck.
203–4. *one of ... trade*] a member of this or that particular guild.
204–5. *Justice ... shire*] the wife of a Justice of the Peace for some particular county.
205–6. *is not ... monuments*] extends beyond our own time, in that we make a mockery of monuments recording the achievements of former ages.
207. *for memory*] to be remembered.

so much worth; so that heretofore virtue was interred in tombs
of gold, now gold is buried with virtue's ensigns.

Poet. No more words. [*He turns towards the Queen.*] We humbly   210
present to your most excellent Majesty this [*presenting the
Queen with an embroidered gown*] as a fitter object for our
arts. For so shallow are we both that the painter must spend his
colours in limning attires, the poet in commending the fashions,
like some witless or bashful wooers that, when they want words   215
to express their passions, are driven to commend the tailor that
made the garment, instead of the mistress that wears it.

[THE END]

210. SD] *This ed.* 211–12. SD] *This ed.; kneeling and offering the gown to the
Queen / Hotson.* 217.1. THE END] *Hotson.*

---

208. *so much worth*] worth a particular amount.
209. *virtue's ensigns*] the insignia of exemplary conduct.
211–12. SD] The record of Caesar's account of the gifts presented to the Queen in
the course of her visit (see p. 110) includes the note that he 'presented her with a Gowne
of Cloth of silver, richly embroidered' (quoted from Hotson, p. 11). The reference to
the tailor that made the garment at lines 216–17 justifies the assumption that it was
the gown that was presented at this point, rather than the other items that Caesar notes.
212–13. *fitter ... arts*] something more suited to our (limited) skills.
214. *limning attires*] depicting elaborate headwear.
commending] celebrating.
215. *want*] lack.

APPENDIX

A COPY OF THE SUPPLICATION DELIVERED TO HER MAJESTY
AT DR CAESAR'S HOUSE, 12TH SEPTEMBER 1598.

Most excellent Lady, I cannot tell whether the owner of this house be subject to stranger passions or fortunes. First drawn out of the world into England in his infancy, taking his name of the sea; in his riper years arbiter of the sea; and now in your realm the eldest judge, the youngest and the poorest, the first a riddle, the last a wonder. For that in all ages it hath been thought rare for judges and executors to be beggars, he covets to strangle time and to make ruins of antiquities. Were I not overawed by the authority he hath over me, I could in a small scroll decipher that which he most coveteth to conceal. His passions proceeding of this unexpected favour that Your Highness vouchsafeth to visit his cell have so possessed

---

2. Dr.] *This ed*; D. Hotson.   2. 12th September] *This ed.*; 12. Septemb. Hotson.

1–31.] Though patently composed at Caesar's instigation, the *supplication* is presented as a device, written on his behalf by a member of his household, unbeknown to Caesar himself.

4–5. *drawn out … infancy*] glossed in the manuscript (in a hand identified by Hotson as Dr Caesar's) as 'before his birth, being yet in his father's loins' (spelling and punctuation modernized for the purposes of this edition).

5. *taking his name of the sea*] Son of Giulio Cesare Adelmare, Caesar took the name Julius Caesar (here enabling the pun on 'sea'), rather than Adelmare as he was occasionally known.

6. *arbiter of the sea*] Caesar was made a general commissioner for piracy in 1581 and a judge of the Admiralty Court in 1584.

eldest] most senior. Caesar had been a judge for eighteen years when the entertainment was composed.

7. *youngest*] possibly an allusion to the fact that Caesar was only 26 when he became a judge.

poorest] Caesar was notorious for his claims of poverty and pursuit of financial advancement.

8. *wonder*] matter of surprise.

9–10. *covets to … antiquities*] i.e. seeks to overthrow historical precedents by his urgent need for financial assistance.

11. *decipher*] unfold.

13. *cell*] cf. the Angler's description of his master's house in *Chiswick* as a 'shed' (see line 3 and line 3n.) and the Dairymaid's scornful account of the Countess of Derby's house at Harefield as a 'pigeon-house', unfit to receive a queen (see Bond, i, p. 492 line 8).

him that, as he lost his name by continuance of time, so now hath he lost his senses by being overjoyed with time; nothing remaining in his memory but this. That his father, physician to Your Highness, was as Martha careful for your body; himself, having the better part, solicitor of your mind. Most happy in both, that Your Majesty hath in your time reposed a trust in them of body and mind.

He presents his heart, his large and wide heart, wherein all the rooms are only taken up for Your Majesty, furnished with no other tapestry than truth, wishing in whose heart that dwelleth not, no heart may dwell in that body. As for your old hostess, joy hath overtaken her with a strange accident – silence. The tongue, which is the heart's herald, is now become ambassador to the heart, where, receiving impressions not to be expressed, itself is turned into heart; so that whensoever hereafter she shall speak, there is no word that proceedeth out of her mouth that shall not be growing fast to the heart. So shall you have her heart's bottom at her tongue's end, and in the meantime her eyes and hands must supply the want of her tongue, till she recover this happy trance.

---

14. *continuance*] the passage.
16. *physician to Your Highness*] Cesare Adelmare (Caesar's father, see line 5n.) was physician to both Mary I and Elizabeth herself.
17. *Martha*] Sister of Mary (possibly Mary Magdalene), Martha is represented in the New Testament as being preoccupied with the domestic responsibilities arising from the arrival of Jesus at their house, whereas Mary was more attentive to his teachings (see Luke, 10.38–42).
18. *solicitor*] one who transacts business on behalf of another (here, as agent of the Crown and hence the Queen's mind). A pun on 'solicitous', paralleling *careful* in the previous line, may also be intended here.
20–2. *He presents ... truth*] Compare *Chiswick*: 'his heart is larger than his house, full of rooms all hung with duty, furnished with prayers, joy, wishes' (lines 31–3).
23. *old*] former. Caesar's wife had entertained the Queen at Mitcham before the death of her previous husband, from whom she had inherited the house.
25. *heart's herald*] spokesman proclaiming the feelings of the heart. For a similar image to the one developed here and in the following lines, see *Cowdray*, lines 29–31.
25. *ambassador*] an envoy.
29. *heart's bottom ... end*] most profound emotions at the tip of her tongue.
31. *recover ... trance*] is cured of this stunned condition induced by good fortune.

THE ENTERTAINMENT AT CHISWICK

INTRODUCTION

At first glance, the entertainment at Sir William Russell's house at Chiswick, performed on 28 and 29 July, during the Queen's truncated summer progress of 1602,[1] hardly merits inclusion in a volume designed to introduce the reader to the scope and variety of Elizabethan progress entertainments. Summed up by Kenneth Muir as 'elegant, brief, and unimportant',[2] it consists of only two speeches, delivered in some unspecified location in the vicinity of the house, and requires nothing more elaborate for its performance than some Angler's accoutrements and a pen. Nevertheless, its discovery in the mid-twentieth century among the documents in the Finch–Hatton Collection,[3] and subsequent publication (ed. Leslie Hotson) in 1953,[4] was a highly significant event. The text, transcribed on a single leaf in 1602, and thus contemporary with the entertainment itself, had been sent to Roger Wilbrahim (Master of Requests)[5] with the author's name, John Lyly, appended at the foot of the page, and it was that attribution that has served to endow the text with a degree of importance wholly disproportionate to either the scale of the entertainment or the novelty of its design.

The leading court dramatist of the 1580s and author of the best-selling prose work of the Elizabethan–Jacobean age, Lyly was thought to have ceased writing around 1590, subsequent to the closure of Paul's Boys (the juvenile troupe for which he customarily wrote), though his earlier prose and dramatic works continued to appear on the bookstalls throughout the 1590s. As noted above (pp. 113–14), no satisfactory explanation had been advanced, prior to the discovery of the *Chiswick* text, of how he employed his time between the dissolution of the company and his death in 1606, though a claim that he continued to provide entertainments for presentation before the Queen had been made by R. Warwick Bond as early as 1902,[6] but had been dismissed on the grounds that it rested on internal evidence alone. The attribution of the *Chiswick* entertainment to him by a contemporary witness, in a document addressed to a recipient in a position to assess the validity of the claim, supplied the external evidence needed to substantiate Bond's position, and added weight to the contention that *The Entertainment at Mitcham*, which came to light in the same year as the *Chiswick* text, was also the dramatist's work (see pp. 113–14 above).[7] Published together in 1953, the two texts reopened the possibility that, rather than disappearing from public view circa 1590, Lyly continued to write for the court throughout the remainder of Elizabeth's reign, encouraging the reconsideration of a series of entertainments previously attributed to him on stylistic grounds alone.[8] While being of minor interest in literary terms, *The Entertainment at Chiswick* may thus be seen as a highly important historical document, simultaneously throwing fresh light on the career of a major early modern writer, while adding a new dimension to the range of insights to be achieved through the study of Elizabethan progress entertainments.

The validity of the unknown copyist's attribution of the entertainment is supported by numerous aspects of the text. As Muir noted in 1953, the work is notable for its elegance, and the characteristic features of the euphuistic mode (the highly patterned style, rooted in antithetical balance, inaugurated in Lyly's first published work) inform every aspect of the text. The welcoming address, delivered in the piscatory tradition by an Angler (cf. *Cowdray*, p. 22 above), unites the presentation of a species of petition (cf. *Mitcham*) with the conventional insistence on the lamentable inadequacy of the host's provisions, with the speech as a whole turning, in a typically Lylian paradox, on the notion of an entirely welcome prospect being productive of dismay. Oppositions, frequently pointed by alliteration and wordplay, as elsewhere in the Lylian corpus, inform the syntactic structure throughout (e.g. 'a swift, but a sweet, whispering', 'not meaning to set down excuses but eye-truths': lines 2 and 6–7), while etymologically unrelated terms are drawn together through eye-rhyme, and syllabic repetition (e.g. 'driven into such a quandary that I quaked', 'neither wind tight not weather tied', 'untrimmed, untiled, unhandsome': lines 4–5, 8, 9). The familiar tropes and stylistic devices combine in an exercise in verbal dexterity designed, like the writer's court comedies, to delight a monarch notable for her own readiness of mind, while images found elsewhere in the Lylian canon further embed the piece in the dramatist's work. The notion that 'Princes' minds are like heaven's dew, falling on shrubs as well as cedars' (lines 20–1), for example, occurs in both *Euphues and His England* (p. 189) and *Campaspe* (5.4.143–4), while the fact that the speaker is an Angler looks back to a host of Lylian compositions in which aspects of fishing are evoked.

It is the relationship between the welcoming speech and the lines delivered on the Queen's departure, however, which speaks most strongly of Lyly's work. The opening proposition 'Here is the world now; when you are gone there is none' (line 36) initiates the opposition underpinning the entirety of the speech between the host's euphoric state of mind during the Queen's visit and his depression of spirit as it draws to a close, developing the inevitability of that reversal through the antithetical structure characteristic of euphuistic prose (cf. 'My Master that yesternight was amazed with joy, is now with grief astonished' (lines 36–8). Once again, contrasts are pointed by syllabic repetition, alliteration, and puns, enforcing the sense of pattern informing the passage as a whole, and thus the inevitability of the experience that it records (cf. 'light'/'lightning', 'a flash and a farewell', 'a night would seem to you a year of wearisomeness, though a year for your abode would have been to him shorter than a night': lines 39, and 42–44). The variation of the Latin quotation from the Gospel according to St Matthew with which the welcoming address came to a close reinforces the parallel between the two speeches and the reversal of feelings that they denote, highlighting the see-saw nature of their relationship, and drawing the two passages into a conceptual whole. Above all, the conventional assertion of the limitations of the host's provisions, developed in the opening lines of the first speech, is given a larger relevance at the close of the second by the description of the richness of the lodging afforded to the monarch in the heart of her host, with the familiar trope emerging, not simply as a straightforward self-deprecating device but as the antithetical counterpart of an assertion of a devotion beyond expression in material terms.

The inclusion of *The Entertainment at Chiswick* in this volume is not solely justified, however, by the interest afforded by its authorship to theatre historians and students of Lyly's work. Its relatively recent discovery precluded its inclusion in either John Nichols's monumental *The Progresses and Public Processions of Queen Elizabeth I* in 1823, or Bond's *The Complete Works of John Lyly* in 1902, and neither the *Mitcham* nor the *Chiswick* entertainment was added to the 2014 revised edition of Nichols's work. The piece has consequently been largely neglected following its initial publication in 1953,[9] and no fully annotated, modern-spelling edition has yet appeared in print. Its neglect has not merely frustrated the study of the later phase of the author's work but has denied access for the majority of readers to a composition which, though unoriginal in terms of the conflicting emotions that it records, has some claim to be regarded, in its unity of subject and style, as the quintessential expression of the sentiments underpinning Elizabethan progress entertainments as a whole.

A NOTE ON THE TEXT

Though, in common with other Elizabethan progress entertainments, the text of the two speeches delivered at Chiswick is known to have circulated in manuscript immediately following the event,[10] the work was lost to view, as noted above, until the mid-twentieth-century when it was discovered in the Finch–Hatton collection (MS Finch Hatton 2414). Only one edition of the piece (ed. Leslie Hotson) has appeared since that time, and, though the manuscript has been independently transcribed for the present edition, it is inevitably heavily dependent on Hotson's work. Editorial practice differs, nevertheless, from Hotson's in a variety of respects (cf. *The Entertainment at Mitcham*, pp. 114–15 above). Spelling and punctuation have been modernized in the interests of greater accessibility, stage directions have been introduced to clarify the action, and through line numbering has been employed throughout, in line with previous items in this edition. The text is more fully annotated than Hotson's, in which the notes are largely concerned with parallels between the piece and other items in the Lylian canon, while the material is presented as an edition of a dramatic work, rather than as a printed version of a document designed to inform a particular recipient of a recent event.[11]

NOTES

1 The progress began with the visit to Chiswick (Middlesex), and proceeded via Harlington (Middlesex), Harefield House (Middlesex), and Burnham (Buckinghamshire) to Oatlands (the Queen's own country house in Surrey), before being cut short by bad weather, and a widespread outbreak of smallpox (see *Nichols*, iv, p. 202).
2 Kenneth Muir, 'Queen Elizabeth's Entertainment at Mitcham' (review article), *Review of English Studies*, NS 5 (1954), p. 408.
3 The manuscript is now in the Northamptonshire Record Office (MS Finch Hatton 2414).
4 The piece was published in conjunction with *The Entertainment at Mitcham*. See Leslie Hotson, ed., *Queen Elizabeth's Entertainment at Mitcham*, Yale Elizabethan Club (New Haven, 1953) and *Mitcham*, Introduction, pp. 113–14 above.
5 No satisfactory explanation has been advanced for the forwarding of the text to Wilbrahim, though copies of Elizabethan entertainments commonly circulated in manuscript during this period (see n. 10).
6 See Bond, i, pp. 404ff.
7 Some slight evidence in support of the attribution may be supplied by the possibility that Russell (born 1553?) and Lyly (born 1554?) may have known one another at Oxford, both having been students at Magdalen.
8 See Leah Scragg, 'Angling for Answers: Looking for Lyly in the 1590s', *Review of English Studies*, NS 67/279 (2015), pp. 237–49.
9 Circulation of the material was also restricted by the limitation of the print run of Hotson's edition to 500 copies.
10 A copy of the text (now lost) was sent by Sir William Browne to Sir Robert Sidney, for example, on 12 August 1602, together with a copy of the entertainment at Harefield (performed from 31 of July to 2 August 1602, following the Queen's visit to Chiswick). See *Progresses*, pp. 238 and 244.
11 Hotson's text concludes, for example, with '[*Endorsed*] To the Right Worshipfull / Roger Wilbraham Esquior / *Master* of Requestes geve these. /' in line with the deleted endorsement on the reverse of the manuscript source.

THE ENTERTAINMENT AT CHISWICK

[*An* ANGLER *with a pen encounters the* QUEEN *on her way to the house.*]

[*Angler.*] As I was fishing for my supper (for the Thames is my shambles) there flew a swift, but a sweet, whispering that the Queen would lodge in my Master's shed – house I cannot call it. I threw my angle one way, and my net another, driven into such a quandary that I quaked. From fishing I fell to writing, how to avoid that I most desired, not meaning to set down excuses but eye-truths. How the house was ruinous, unaired, and by the absence of the owner, kept neither wind tight nor weather tied; untrimmed, untiled, unhandsome, and so unfit to circle in that Majesty which the world can scarce enclose that I feared the sight would breed dislike, the entrance discontent, the lodging contempt.

So long I wrestled with my wits to excuse my Master that yourself was within kenning, and then I knew not how to excuse myself; for my Master snatched the pen from me, commanding me to deliver it to your Majesty, with a most humble entreaty to ask a pardon of you for all offences, oversights, defects, or

---

0.1–2. SD] *This ed.*   1. SP] *This ed.*   8. tied] *This ed.*; tide MS.

HT] For the circumstances surrounding the Queen's visit to Sir William Russell at Chiswick, see Introduction, p. 132 n. 1.
   CHISWICK] then a small village on the Thames, largely inhabited by fishermen and their families. The occupation of the speaker of the two addresses is thus appropriate for the location.
   1–2. *shambles*] place where meat (and occasionally fish) is sold.
   3. *my Master's*] i.e. Sir William Russell's.
   shed] For comparable assertions of the modesty of the host's residence, see *Elvetham*, line 255 and 255n.
   6–7. *excuses ... eye-truths*] For a similar play on the names of the letters of the alphabet (here X and I), see *Mother Bombie*: '*Dromio.* Everyone remember his cue. / *Risio.* Ay, and his K, or else we shall thrive ill' (2.4.22–3).
   7. *eye-truths*] that which is evident to the eye.
   8. *weather tied*] made secure against the weather.
   9. *untrimmed*] undecorated.
   14. *yourself*] i.e. the Queen.
   kenning] sight (with a possible play on 'ken', a house used by disreputable persons, sustaining the notion that the accommodation is unfit for a queen).

discontentments that this rusty and unrepaired cottage might offer, and with this pen to sign it. [*He presents the pen to the Queen.*] This he bad me add: that Princes' minds are like heaven's dew, falling on shrubs as well as cedars; that goddesses will not be gainsaid their pleasures and wills, being harbingers to billet themselves where they list, under the roofs of palaces or penthouses. As his joys are without measure, so he hopes they will be without end, for he knows no comfort to be compared with this, that in your Highness's heart there should be left the least thought or memory of one so absolutely divided from the court and from himself that, the stock being dead, you vouchsafe to breathe favour on the branches. Here his joy is enlarged, that all his friends may impart of it.

And thus he willed me to conclude in all humility; that his heart is larger than his house, full of rooms all hung with duty, furnished with prayers, joy, wishes, yet saying with the Centurion, '*Non sum dignus*'.

[*The* ANGLER'S *speech*] *at her Majesty's departure.*

[Angler.] Here is the world now; when you are gone there is none. My Master, that yesternight was amazed with joy, is now with grief astonished. In his judgement he foretold his fortunes: that happiness would light on him like lightning, a flash and a farewell;

19–20. SD] *This ed.* 35.] Bracketed material this ed. 36. SP] *This ed.*

20–1. *Princes' minds ... cedars*] variant form of an analogy repeatedly deployed in Lyly's work. Compare *England*: 'The name of a prince is like the sweet dew which falleth as well upon low shrubs as high trees' (p. 189), and *Campaspe*: 'Love falleth like dew as well upon the low grass as upon the high cedar' (5.4.143–4).

22. *gainsaid*] denied.

harbingers] those sent ahead to purvey lodging for a royal train (referring back to *pleasures and wills* in the same line).

23. *list*] wish.

24. *penthouses*] low-quality structures with sloping roofs appended to other buildings.

27–8. *so absolutely ... himself*] obscure. The comment may allude to the failure of Russell's aggressive policy in Ireland and recall to London in 1597.

28–9. *the stock ... branches*] Russell's father, the second Earl of Bedford, died in 1585 and his elder brothers in 1572, 1584, and 1585. His nephew, Edward Russell, third Earl of Bedford, was implicated in the Essex rebellion of 1601.

34. Non sum dignus] abbreviated form of the Centurion's response to Christ's offer to come to his house to heal his sick servant: '*Non sum dignus ut intres sub tectum meum*' ('I am not worthy that thou shouldst come under my roof': Matthew, 8.8).

36. *Here ... now*] i.e. the entire world is comprised in the monarch's presence.

37–8. *amazed ... astonished*] overwhelmed with wonder / stunned (as with dismay).

that beauty and virtue could not be pent in a pigeon-cote but 40
would burst out into a wider air, though into no larger heart;
that a night would seem to you a year of wearisomeness, though
a year for your abode would have been to him shorter than a
night. Wheresoever you go, happy may the place be. His thoughts
shall fly after, as faithfully as any's for devotion, though not so 45
fortunate for entertainment. *Non fuit dignus.*

---

40. *pent in a pigeon-cote*] shut up in a pigeon house (cf. modern English 'dovecote').
43. *abode*] stay.
44. *His*] i.e. William Russell's.
46. *for entertainment*] in being able to entertain her.
Non fuit dignus] He was not worthy (with a play on *Non sum dignus* at line 34).

INDEX

Page numbers refer to the Introduction or the prefatory material to a specific text; 'n' following a page reference indicates the page on which the cue to the note signified by the ensuing number may be found. The title of an entertainment followed by a line number denotes the location of the headword in the specified text. Individual words appearing in various inflected forms are usually grouped under one form; phrases are indexed in the form in which they appear in the text. Where a gloss is repeated in the annotations, only the initial occurrence is recorded.

abode *Elvetham* line 117, *Bisham* line 124
abruptly *Elvetham* line 377
abstract, absolute *Mitcham* line 101
Adelmare, Giulio Cesare *Mitcham* Appendix lines 5n., 16n.
admiration *Mitcham* line 130
Albion *Elvetham* line 420
amazed *Mitcham* line 80
amiable *Mitcham* line 60
Answerable *Elvetham* line 613
Apelles *Mitcham* line 77
argues *Elvetham* line 225
arms *Cowdray* line 111
ask reason of reason *Mitcham* line 45
astonishment *Mitcham* line 131
attire and the countenance *Mitcham* line 93
Augusta *Elvetham* line 217n.
Aureola *Elvetham* line 660
avail *Elvetham* line 551
Ay *Bisham* line 59

babies *Mitcham* line 82
Bales, Peter p. 113, *Mitcham* lines 16–17n.
bandore *Elvetham* line 677
banquet *Elvetham* line 607

Barley, William p. 24n.21
Barnes, Joseph pp. 9n.27, 92, 98
bass-viol *Elvetham* line 677
Baucis *see* Philemon
beck *Cowdray* line 107, *Elvetham* line 256
being advertised *Elvetham* line 352
bereaven, of power *Bisham* line 143
Bisham Abbey pp. 6, 7, 92, *Bisham* line 1n.
  Entertainment at pp. 4, 5, 6, 9, 10, 13, 91–108, *Cowdray* lines 86–8n.
board-and-cord p. 49, *Elvetham* line 603
Bond, R. Warwick pp. 5n.17, 25, 26n.27, 55, 96, 98, 114, 132, 134, *Elvetham* lines 255n., 547n., *Mitcham* lines 16–17n., *Mitcham* Appendix line 13n.
borders, board a pair of *Mitcham* line 202
bottom *Elvetham* line 46
Breton, Nicholas p. 4
Bristol, progress to p. 2n.5
Browne, Sir Anthony *Cowdray* line 38n.
Browne, Sir William p. 134n.10

INDEX

Brydges, Samuel Egerton p. 98
bulrush *Elvetham* line 422
Butler, Katherine pp. 13, 20n.10, 22nn.14, 15, 24n.19, 50n.9
buttery *Elvetham* line 38

Caesar, Sir Julius pp. 8, 110–11, 114, *Mitcham* Appendix *passim*
canopy of estate *Elvetham* lines 341–2
canvassing the heavens *Mitcham* line 55
car *Bisham* line 154
Carey, Sir George *Elvetham* line 349
carman *Mitcham* line 62
carps / carpers *Cowdray* line 241
carried *Elvetham* line 36
Caryll, Sir John *Cowdray* line 284
cast *Mitcham* line 20
Cecil, William p. 22n.15
Ceres *Bisham* line 129
chambers *Elvetham* line 304
Chambers, E.K (*The Elizabethan Stage*) pp. 2n.8, 3n.11, *Cowdray* line 43n.
chandlery *Elvetham* line 28
cheer, store of his *Elvetham* lines 309–10
Chiswick pp. 5, 6, 132n.1
  Entertainment at pp. 2n.4, 5, 6, 9, 10, 113–14, 131–8, *Elvetham* line 255n., *Mitcham* Appendix lines 13n., 20–2n.
cithern *Elvetham* line 677
civility *Bisham* line 19
Clarke, Sir William p. 49n.8
close *Bisham* line 107
Closewalks Wood *Cowdray* lines 8on., 187–8n.
clouts, pricking of *Bisham* lines 29–30
colouring, admitteth no *Mitcham* line 114
comfits *Elvetham* line 648
comfortable *Elvetham* line 299

compass *Elvetham* line 8
Conceit *Bisham* line 138
conceives *Mitcham* line 57
congers *Elvetham* line 640
contemn *Bisham* line 8
contemned *Bisham* line 159
continuance *Mitcham* Appendix line 14
conveniency *Elvetham* line 5
conveyed myself *Mitcham* line 6
cop height *Cowdray* lines 134–5
copy, change my *Mitcham* line 40
cornets *Elvetham* line 364, *Bisham* line 1
Corydon and Phillida *Elvetham* line 565
counter *Elvetham* line 611
Coventry, Queen's visit to p. 2
Cowdray pp. 3n.9, 4, 7, 10, 18, 92
  curse on *Cowdray* line 20n.
  Entertainment at pp. 4, 5, 7, 7n.20, 9, 10, 11, 12, 13, 17–43, *Mitcham* Appendix line 25n.
cries, London *Mitcham* line 196
cross *Elvetham* line 232
cry *Cowdray* line 180
cry grigs in the street *Mitcham* line 34
cunningly *Elvetham* line 433
curious *Elvetham* line 607
current *Mitcham* line 116
curstness *Bisham* line 43

darts *Elvetham* line 473
dash over the head, hath a *Mitcham* line 90
Davidson, Peter and Stevenson, Jane pp. 92n.3., 94n.6, 95n.10, 96n.14, 97n.18, 98n.22, *Bisham* line 1n.
Davies, H. Neville pp. 4n.13, 5n.15, 14, 47n.5, 48n.6., 52, 55, *Elvetham* lines 12–13n., 317n., 364n., 643n., 648n., 676n.

INDEX

decipher *Mitcham* Appendix line 11
deck *Elvetham* line 292
deluded *Elvetham* line 594
Dent, Alice p. 110n.5
    Alderman John *Mitcham* p. 110n.5
Detur dignissimae Elvetham line 495
dight *Elvetham* line 286
divers *Cowdray* line 150
divisions, excellent *Elvetham* line 435
Dormer, Lady Elizabeth *Cowdray* line 38
dotterels *Bisham* line 52
double *Bisham* line 76
double stitch *Bisham* line 70
draught *Cowdray* line 217
dread *Elvetham* line 458

Eastbourne Priory *Cowdray* line 77n.
Echo *Bisham* line 11
Egerton, Sir Thomas p. 3n.11
eglantine *Bisham* line 73
Elvetham *Entertainment at* pp. 3, 3n.10, 4, 5, 6, 7, 8, 9, 10, 11, 13, 14, 45–89, *Cowdray* lines 43n., 77n., 180n., *Bisham* lines 132.1n., 146n.
England's Helicon p. 5, *Elvetham* lines 278–93n., 570–97n., *Bisham* line 132.1
ensigns, virtue's *Mitcham* line 209
envy *Bisham* line 6
envy at *Elvetham* line 264
Erasmus (*Apophthegmata*) *Cowdray* lines 240–1n.
escutcheons *Cowdray* line 112
ewery *Elvetham* line 28
excuses / eye-truths *Chiswick* lines 6–7

fair law *Cowdray* lines 72–3
Fame, golden trump of *Elvetham* line 459
Fellowes, Edmund H. (*The English Madrigal*) p. 55

fetters, leading affections in *Bisham* line 93
Finch Hatton Collection pp. 132, 134
fingers' ends, invention pinned to the *Mitcham* lines 19–20
firewheels *Elvetham* line 617
fishing for commodity *Cowdray* line 196
flanker *Elvetham* line 51
flat-work *Elvetham* line 643
fond *Cowdray* line 60
froward passing *Cowdray* line 101

gainsaid *Chiswick* line 22
galled *Cowdray* line 68
Gilling Castle *Cowdray* line 112n.
Glaucus *Elvetham* line 362
Glemham, Sir Henry *Cowdray* line 283
Globe Education p. 1n.1
golden age *Elvetham* line 491
Goldring, Elizabeth pp. 5n.16, 19n.8
Goring, Sir Henry *Cowdray* line 282
Gough, Richard p. 54
Graces, the *Elvetham* line 251
Greene, Robert (*James IV*) *Cowdray* lines 227–8n.
Greg, W.W. p. 55
Grey, Sir Henry *Elvetham* line 348
Grey, Katherine p. 47
grigs *see* cry
grizzly *Elvetham* line 359

hale *Elvetham* line 426
hand, enforced by *Elvetham* lines 628–9
handy *Elvetham* line 46
happily *Elvetham* line 270
happy *Cowdray* line 18
harbingers *Chiswick* line 22
Harefield, *Entertainment at* pp. 5, 6, 110n.4, 132n.1, 134n.10, *Cowdray* lines 227–8n., *Elvetham* line 255n., *Mitcham* Appendix line 13n.

INDEX

Harlington p. 132n.1
harness *Bisham* line 99
Heal, Felicity p. 110n.4
Heale, Elizabeth pp. 18n.6, 21n.13, 23n.16
heart's herald *Mitcham* Appendix line 25
heart's-ease *Bisham* line 73
hearts of oak *Cowdray* line 124
Heaton, Gabriel pp. 2n.7, 18n.4, 18n.7, 24n.17, 25, 26n.27, *Cowdray* lines 112n., 187–8n., 191n.
Heedless *Bisham* line 107
held up *Elvetham* line 330
Henry VIII, King, will of *Elvetham* p. 47n.1
heroical verse *Elvetham* line 111
heronshaws *Elvetham* line 635
Hertford, Countess of *Elvetham* lines 295–6
  Earl of pp. 47, 53–4
Hoby, Sir Edward pp. 92, 94n.7
homely *Mitcham* line 99
Homer *Elvetham* line 427n., *Mitcham* line 90 (*Homere*)
Hotson, Leslie pp. 110, 111, 113, 114–15, 132, 134–5, *Mitcham* lines 211–12n., *Mitcham* Appendix lines 4–5n.
Hungerford, Sir Walter *Elvetham* lines 348–9
Hunnis, William p. 4
Hunsdon, Henry Carey Lord p. 18
Hunter, G.K pp. 24n.18, 25, 114

Ibis Homere prae Mitcham line 90
imperial crown *Elvetham* line 655
India *Elvetham* line 410
insult *Elvetham* line 509
invention *Mitcham* line 72
invention, hatched *Mitcham* line 12

Johnson, Edward p. 4, *Elvetham* line 676n.

Jones, Robert (*The Muses' Garden for Delights*) p. 24n.21
jugging *Mitcham* line 61
jugglings, unchaste *Bisham* line 85
Jupiter, tree of *Cowdray* line 132
just *Elvetham* line 2

Kenilworth p. 2
  Princely Pleasures at pp. 6, 7–8, *Cowdray* lines 6–33n.
kenning *Chiswick* line 14
Kent, progress through p. 2n.5
kept strait *Cowdray* line 153
Kesson, Andy p. 5n.14
Kildare, Countess of *Cowdray* line 50
kind *Elvetham* line 310
King's College Chapel p. 1n.1
King Edward VI School, Stratford p. 1n.1
Kinney, Arthur F. p. 8n.22, *Elvetham* lines 190–2n.

larded *Mitcham* line 62
lardery *Elvetham* line 28
largesse *Elvetham* line 560
lawn *Cowdray* line 73
lays *Elvetham* line 454
leaches *Elvetham* line 648
Leicester, Earl of pp. 2, 4, 7
limbecks *Mitcham* line 49
limned out so lively *Mitcham* line 25
limning attires *Mitcham* line 214
loureth *Bisham* line 140
lowering *Cowdray* line 209
lumps *Cowdray* line 265
Lyly pp. 4, 25–6, 96–77, 98, 113–14, 132–4, *Mitcham*, lines 16–17n.
  Campaspe p. 113, *Cowdray* line 12n., *Bisham* lines 33–4n., *Mitcham* lines 61n., 95–9n., 108–9n., 112n., *Chiswick* lines 20–1n.

INDEX

Endymion p. 6, *Elvetham* line 395n.
Euphues: The Anatomy of Wit Cowdray lines 174–7n.
Euphues and His England pp. 7n.18, 25n.26, 95, 112, *Cowdray* lines 199–201n., *Elvetham* line 648n., *Bisham* lines 49–50n., *Mitcham* lines 13n.,127n., 187n., *Chiswick* lines 20–1n.
Galatea p. 1n.1, *Cowdray* line 223n., *Bisham* lines 70–1n., 93–4n.
Midas Cowdray lines 100–1n., *Bisham* lines 126–7, *Mitcham* line 187n.
Mother Bombie p. 25.n.26, *Cowdray* lines 107–8n., 235–6n., *Bisham* lines 62–3n., *Mitcham* lines 75–6n., 90n., *Chiswick* lines 6–7n.
Pap with an Hatchet p. 25n.26, *Cowdray* lines 235–6n.
Sappho and Phao Cowdray line 223n.
The Woman in the Moon p. 4, *Elvetham* lines 512–15n.

maids *Cowdray* line 220
malice *Elvetham* line 264
March–panes *Elvetham* line 645
marmalets *Elvetham* line 648
Martin Marprelate p. 26
Martyn Joseph (*New Epigrams*) pp. 111–12
Marvyn, Sir James *Elvetham* line 349
Mary, Queen of Scots p. 18, *Bisham* line 107n.
Masque of the Muses, The p. 96
Master of Requests p. 111, *Mitcham* line 2
measure *Elvetham* line 653

meat *Bisham* line 38
Meres, Francis pp. 48n.7, 97
mice *Bisham* line 44
Midas p. 94n.5
Milton, John (*Comus*) *Elvetham* line 653n.
Mitcham p. 112
  Entertainment at pp. 1n.4, 5, 6(2), 7, 9, 10(2), 95, 109–29, 132n.4, 133, 134, *Elvetham* lines 210–12n., 435n., 453–4n., *Bisham* lines 93–4n.
Montague, Anthony Browne, Viscount pp. 3, 7n.20, 18–20, 23, 92
Morley, Thomas pp. 4, 50 *Elvetham* lines 321–2
Muir, Kenneth pp. 114, 132, 133
Munday, Anthony p. 97
mussel shells *Mitcham* line 19
mystery *Bisham* line 37

Nashe, Thomas (*Summer's Last Will and Testament*) p. 5
Neaera *Elvetham* line 68
Nereus *Elvetham* line 67
Netters *Cowdray* line 211
nibbling *Cowdray* line 193
Nichols, John pp. 54–5
noble *Cowdray* line 218
Non fuit dignus Chiswick line 46
Non sum dignus Chiswick line 34
Norfolk, progress through p. 2n.5
Northampton Record Office p. 132n.3
note above *e la*, set a *Mitcham* line 187

ochre *Mitcham* line 89
odds *Bisham* line 75, *Mitcham* line 154
Odiham *Elvetham* line 101
O'Farrell, Nellie McNeill p. 110
offices *Elvetham* line 16
orderly set *Elvetham* line 50

ordinary guess p. 47, *Elvetham* lines 12–13
Ovid
Ams Amatoria Elvetham line 188n.
Heroides Cowdray line 223n.
Metamorphoses p. 94n.5, *Elvetham* lines 206–7n., *Bisham* lines 126–7n.

packing, be *Bisham* lines 80–1
Pan *Bisham* line 5
paragone debate pp. 4, 111–12
Parker, Sir Nichols *Cowdray* lines 285, 287n.
particulate *Elvetham* line 309
passing amiable *Cowdray* line 18
pastes *Elvetham* line 648
pastime *Elvetham* line 557
Paul's Boys p. 114
pavans *Elvetham* line 321
peak over the perch *Cowdray* lines 244–5
Peele, George (*The Judgement of Paris*) p. 10n.28
pendants *Elvetham* line 60
peremptory *Mitcham* line 3
Philemon and Baucis, pp. 6–7, *Elvetham* lines 206–7n., *Bisham* line 109n.
Phorcus *Elvetham* line 362
pieces *Elvetham* lines 59, 305
pigeon-cote, pent in a *Chiswick* line 40
pikes of pleasure *Elvetham* lines 617–18
pinnace *Elvetham* line 58
pistol-proof, words of *Mitcham* line 55
playing *Elvetham* line 492
plenty, ornament of my *Bisham* line 157
Plutarch *Cowdray* lines 240–1n.
point of war *Elvetham* line 521
Pomona *Bisham* line 134

pompous array *Elvetham* line 354
Porter, Chloe pp. 13–14, 111n.10
porters *Cowdray* line 7
posy *Mitcham* line 88
pot *Mitcham* line 32
practise *Cowdray* line 157
presence seat *Elvetham* line 66
presently *Elvetham* line 341
prime *Elvetham* line 441
privy *Cowdray* line 269
prize the worth *Mitcham* line 143
prodigal, paint the ... beard *Mitcham* lines 84–5
prodigious *Bisham* line 5
proportion of *Cowdray* lines 42–3
prospect of, under the *Elvetham* line 303
prove *Mitcham* line 137
Purcell, Henry p. 5n.15

quality *Elvetham* line 227
Queen's stitch p. 95, *Bisham* line 73

rampired *Cowdray* line 127
Read Not Dead, p. 1n.1
ready *Elvetham* line 651
receipt, of no great *Elvetham* line 9
record *Elvetham* line 289
request, be in *Mitcham* line 83
retire *Elvetham* line 712
Revels, Office of the p. 4
right *Bisham* line 74
rive asunder *Bisham* line 154
Room of Estate *Elvetham* line 22
Roses *Bisham* line 73
Ross, Sarah p. 96, *Bisham* line 23n.
rough-hewed *Cowdray* line 96
Russell, Anne pp. 94, 96, *Bisham* lines 23n., 116–18n.
Russell, Lady Elizabeth pp. 92, 94–8, *Bisham* lines 1n., 23n., 116–18n., 164n.

INDEX

Russell, Elizabeth pp. 94, 95n.9, *Bisham* lines 23n., 116–18
Russell Edward, third Earl of Bedford *Chiswick* lines 28–9n.
Russell, Lord John p. 92n.2
Russell, Sir William p. 132, *Chiswick* lines 27–8n.

St Matthew's festival *Elvetham* line 326
saffron *Elvetham* line 469
samplers *Bisham* line 24
scallop shells *Cowdray* line 82
sciences, seven liberal *Mitcham* lines 172–3
Scottish jigs *Elvetham* line 365
Scragg, Leah pp. 4n.12, 25n.25, 96n.17, 114n.16, 133n.8
sempsters *Mitcham* line 194
Seymour, Edward, Earl of Hertford pp. 47, 53–4
Shakespeare, William
  2HIV Mitcham line 55n.
  KL Bisham lines 57–8n.
  LLL p. 113
  MND p. 5, *Bisham* line 73n.
  Tim p. 111
  TN Bisham line 44n.
shambles *Chiswick* lines 1–2
shed *Chiswick* line 3
shell, air-enforcing *Elvetham* line 485
Sheriff of the Shire *Cowdray* line 287
Sibyl *Elvetham* line 541
Sidney, Sir Philip *Bisham* line 103n.
  An Apology for Poetry p.111, *Elvetham* lines 118–119n.
  The Lady of May pp. 4, 6, 8, 8n.23
Sidney, Sir Robert p. 134n.10
silly *Elvetham* line 592
singular in *Mitcham* line 159
slubberest up *Mitcham* lines 20–1
Sneyd Consort p. 56n.12
solicitor *Mitcham* Appendix line 18
sounded *Cowdray* line 5

span *Cowdray* line 90
Spanish Armada p. 18, *Cowdray* lines 128n., 136–8n., *Elvetham* lines 214n., 381n., 404n., 419n., 547n.
Spenser, Edmund
  The Fairie Queeene pp. 4, 96n.13, *Elvetham* line 653n.
  The Shepheardes Calender p. 6
spent *Elvetham* line 615
spoil *Elvetham* line 420
springe *Bisham* line 51
staunch *Cowdray* line 237
stayed *Cowdray* line 16
stayeth *Cowdray* line 206
Stevenson, Jane *see* Davidson, Peter
stout *Bisham* line 9
Strong, Roy
  The Cult of Elizabeth p. 95n.11
  'Depicting Gloriana' pp. 7n.18, 95n.12
suckades *Elvetham* line 648
sudden, on the *Elvetham* line 6
sufferance, old *Elvetham* line 501
suffered *Elvetham* lines 517–18
sufficing *Elvetham* line 5
sugar-work *Elvetham* line 626
suitors *Elvetham* line 33
sumptuary laws *Cowdray* line 155n.
surer *Cowdray* line 124
Sylvanus *Elvetham* line 76

taffeta sarcenet *Elvetham* line 268
tapster *Mitcham* line 32
teen *Elvetham* line 462
tennis *Elvetham* line 601
Theobalds *Cowdray* line 112n.
  Queen's visit to p. 3n.9, *Elvetham* lines 14–16n.
Thetis *Elvetham* line 427
Tilley, Morris Palmer *Cowdray* lines 99–100n., 174–7n., 204–5n., 227–8n., 235–6n., *Bisham* lines 49–50n., 51n., 53n., *Mitcham* lines 13n., 41nn., 75–6n., 122n.

Tobias *Mitcham* lines 85–7n.
toils *Elvetham* line 245
tongue's mew *Cowdray* lines 107–8
towards *Elvetham* line 352
toy *Bisham* line 166
train *Elvetham* line 383
treble-viol *Elvetham* line 677
trip *Bisham* line 119
Tritons *Elvetham* line 358
Troy, second *Elvetham* line 282
Tymme, Thomas p. 112

ugly *Elvetham* line 371
una Elvetham line 141
unacquainted *Elvetham* line 204
unchristened *Mitcham* line 53
ut pictura poesis p. 111

valanced about *Elvetham* line 345
verdure *Elvetham* line 417
Virgil
 Aeneid Cowdray lines 34–5n.
 Eclogues Cowdray line 160n.,
  Elvetham lines 244–6n.
Virgin Queen, cult of p. 7
virtue *Bisham* line 26
vouchsafe/vouchsafed *Cowdray*
 lines 66/29

Wade no further *Mitcham* line 39
Walsingham, Francis p. 18n.2

Wanstead p. 6
 Entertainment at pp. 4, 5n.16,
  8(3)
wanton *Elvetham* line 491
wanton fire *Elvetham* line 507
wares *Mitcham* line 31
Watson, Thomas pp. 4, 48 (2),
 Elvetham lines 123–89n.,
 278–93n.
weeds *Elvetham* line 292
whist *Bisham* line 116
Whyte, Rowland p. 96n.15
Wilbraham, Roger p. 135n.11
wild-fire *Elvetham* line 382
Wild Man pp. 93, 95, *Cowdray*
 line 113, *Bisham* line 2
Wilson, Jean pp. 8, 20n.11, 26n.27,
 97, 98, *Cowdray* lines 47n.,
 191n.
Windsor, Royal Library at p. 55
wink *Cowdray* line 23
woodcocks *Bisham* line 51
Woodstock, the entertainment at
 p. 8n.24
Worcester, progress to p. 2n.5
worms *Elvetham* line 638

Yale Elizabethan Club
 p. 114n.17

Zeusis *Mitcham* line 127n.

EU authorised representative for GPSR:
Easy Access System Europe, Mustamäe tee 50,
10621 Tallinn, Estonia
gpsr.requests@easproject.com

www.ingramcontent.com/pod-product-compliance
Lightning Source LLC
Chambersburg PA
CBHW021859230426
43671CB00006B/448